Ye Brick Church of 1639 Restored

Copyright, 1903, by Samuel H. Yonge.

The Site of Old "James Towne" 1607-1698

THE SITE OF OLD "JAMES TOWNE"
1607 ❧❧ 1698

A Brief Historical and
Topographical Sketch

OF THE

First American Metropolis.

Illustrated with Original Maps,

Drawings and Photographs

BY

SAMUEL H. YONGE

"Redivivum est ex vetusto renovatum."—FESTUS.

TERCENTENARY EDITION.

WILDSIDE PRESS

TERCENTENARY EDITION.

"THE Site of Old 'James Towne,' 1607-1698," originally appeared in four consecutive issues of the Virginia Magazine of History and Biography, between January and October, 1904. The monograph was published in book form by the Association for the Preservation of Virginia Antiquities in the same year. The work included the results of the author's original investigations as to the town's site, and was issued to correct the erroneous opinions on the subject, that obtained up to the time of its publication.

The newly discovered matter comprised the locations of the shore line of the head of Jamestown Island in the seventeenth century and several other important topographical features, the site of the former town, including its churches, state house buildings and forts, the probable landing place of the first party of settlers and the residences and grounds of some of the town's prominent people. The determination of these features has been generally accepted. It is disappointing, however, to find that some of the most important original deductions have appeared in other writings, without the customary credit being accorded to "The Site of Old 'James Towne.'"

Since the first publication of the work, no information has been discovered to throw additional light on the subject. After a careful review of the available data and a study of the Ambler MSS., it appears that no change can be made in the map, as originally constructed from the transcripts of the old patents at Richmond, Va.

The text of the present edition is almost identically the same as the first. The exceptions to the above are of a minor character, consisting of the amplification of a few paragraphs to make them clearer, and the addition of two chapters, one a brief outline of some of the social and economic conditions that obtained in England and Virginia during the Jamestown period, the other a connected summary of important events that occurred during the town's life.

The portraits of Sir Henry Wriothsley and Lord La Warr are taken from Brown's *Genesis of the United States,* and that of Sir Edwin Sandys from Brown's *First Republic,* with the sanction of the publishers, Messrs. Houghton, Mifflin and Company, for which courtesy acknowledgment is hereby made.

The tercentenary edition is presented in response to numerous requests, and to meet the demand for information on the subject of the first English settlement in America, arising from the interest awakened by the celebration of its three hundredth anniversary.

It should be a cause for congratulation to those who feel an interest in the preservation of the historic site of Jamestown to know that in January, 1906, the protection of the part of the island bank exposed to the attack of the James River was completed by extending the sea wall, constructed in 1901, to a point where, according to the author's investigations, was situated the southeastern corner of the palisades which inclosed the ancient fort town.

Grateful acknowledgment is hereby made of the valuable assistance rendered by Mr. Frank D. Beckham, of Prince William County, Virginia, in the preparation of this edition, also to Mr. Wm. G. Stanard, the erudite Secretary of the Virginia Historical Society, for many favors, and his encouragement and support.

CONTENTS

CONTENTS.

ILLUSTRATIONS

The Site of Old "James Towne,"
(1607-1698)

BY SAMUEL H. YONGE.

INTRODUCTION.

IT was the author's privilege to have charge, under the direction of the United States Engineer Department in 1900 and 1901, of the work of protecting Jamestown Island from the encroachments of James River.

Before proceeding with the above work an attempt was made to learn the cause and extent of the encroachments. The former was soon discovered to be abrasion by wave action, while the latter, on account of the available evidence being meager and uncertain, could not be satisfactorily determined.

The abraded area at first appeared to be upwards of fifty acres, having its greatest width, about three-eighths of a mile, at the northwestern extremity of the island.

While the protection work was under construction new evidence offered, in the light of which the above area appeared too large. This led to making personal researches among all available sources of information, which occupied the leisure moments of a period of two years.

The results of the above investigation, with regard to the site of the former town, presented in the accompanying monograph, are at variance with the statements of other modern writers.

There are but two descriptions available of the island and town after the latter had passed beyond the transitional stage of a military post, by writers of the time having a personal knowledge of the localities; one by an anonymous writer in about

1676, the other ten years later by the Rev. John Clayton. Both descriptions are quite incomplete. Supplemented by information from other sources, however, they have considerable value, especially that by Mr. Clayton.

In the description of the town by Mr. Richard Randolph, the antiquarian, published in 1849, in the *Virginia Historical Register,* Vol. II, pages 138 and 139, occurs the following:

" I will only add that the great body of the town, which, however, was never very large, was certainly west of the Old Steeple still visible, and is now entirely, or very nearly, submerged in the river. This is clearly proved by the old deeds for lots in the town recorded in the office of James City County Court, which call for bounds that are now under water, and more palpably, by vast numbers of broken bricks and other relics of building that may still be seen in the western bank at low tide."

It is evident from the above quotation that Mr. Randolph was not aware of the fact now disclosed that after about 1623 the greater part of the village was east of the tower ruin. The reasons for his belief that almost the entire town was west of the ruin were probably the following: During about the last three and a half decades of the town's existence the public buildings, as will be shown in the following pages, were west of the tower, on which fact, no doubt, the tradition was founded that the whole town was in that neighborhood; and, as only the western bank of the island was subsequently attacked by the waves, and consequently the foundations of former buildings of that quarter alone were exposed to view by abrasion of the bank, the above tradition was apparently confirmed; further, after the last state house and other buildings were burned in 1698, the standing parts of buildings in the entire town were, in the course of time, obliterated by the town site being put under cultivation and the brick formerly composing the buildings being removed; and, finally, on account of the long interval—a century and a half— between the town's abandonment as the seat of government, by which its few inhabitants, composed principally of resident state officials and tavern keepers, were compelled to remove, and that of a revival of any very great interest in the town, the traditions depended on for fixing its position had become dim and defective.

From what follows it appears that writers of later date than Mr. Randolph accepted and reflected his views, without proper investigation.

According to Bishop Meade, in his *Old Churches and Families of Virginia,* Vol. I, page 111, the town was situated between the existing tower ruin and the upper extremity of the island, its eastern end being a short distance (one hundred and fifty yards) above the ruin, which he places at about a mile below the northern end of the isthmus. He also states in effect that the part of the island above alluded to had been encroached on by the river, thereby implying that the greater part of the town site had been washed away, and that traces of the town were visible at low tide in front of the island bank, *i. e.,* the western bank, which was the part abraded.

From the brief description of the town by the late Edward Duffield Neill, D. D., contained on page 203, *Virginia Carolorum,* published in 1886, it would appear that he, too, believed it to have been at the western extremity of the island. He also states that the quarter called "the New Towne" had been destroyed by the encroachments of the river.

Dr. John Fiske informs us in *Virginia and Her Neighbors,* Vol. II, page 120, published in 1896, that more than half of the town site has been destroyed.

The deductions of Dr. Lyon Gardner Tyler regarding the location of the town site, as set forth in the first edition of *The Cradle of the Republic* are in line with those of other authors.

The unquestioned views of the above-mentioned writers that the town was west of the church tower ruin and that the greater part of it had been engulfed by the river were accepted as correct in beginning the investigation of the subject. As no information was available in historical works as to the extent and shape of the abrasion of the island shore, a study was made of the old records of seventeenth century land grants at

"James Citty." From these grants, principally, it was learned that the town bordered not only the western shore of the island immediately above the tower, but also the adjacent southern shore below for a greater distance, with a total frontage on the river of about three-fourths of a mile.

The patents also show that the quarter of the town referred to in them as the " New Towne " was of a permanent and not of an ephemeral character, and that for many years after its establishment, about 1623, was the most important part of the corporation. The most notable events and incidents of the first two and last three decades of the town's history, however, occurred at and west of the church still marked by the tower ruin.

The Cradle of the Republic is the only work in which an attempt is made to describe the location of the town. On pages 19 and 40 of that work (the first edition) the Back Street of " The New Towne " is placed on a ridge about 250 yards northwesterly from the tower ruin, and on pages 53 and 54, a one-acre tract acquired by William Sherwood in 1681 and a tract belonging to Henry Hartwell in 1688 are located in the same vicinage. If these locations were correct, the town must always have been west of the tower ruin. In the following chapters it will be shown that " The New Towne " with its " Back Street," probably so named on account of being back from the water front or behind the town, and Sherwood's and Hartwell's lots, were east, instead of west of the tower ruin, and towards the eastern end of the town. The Hartwell tract, as shown on the " Map of Iames Citty " accompanying, was about five hundred yards east of the tower, on the southern water front, instead of two hundred and fifty yards west, as given by Dr. Tyler in the above-mentioned work.

In the description of the town during Sir Thomas Gates' first term (1611), Vol. II, page 529, *Economic History of Virginia in the Seventeenth Century,* by Philip Alexander Bruce, the building of a bridge is construed to mean that the structure connected the island with the mainland. This would have created an easy means for the Indians to reach the island and attack the settlers. As will be shown further on, the "bridge" was merely a wharf.

According to Bishop Meade, in his *Old Churches and Families of Virginia,* the island was connected with the mainland by a causeway on the site of the former isthmus about the middle of the eighteenth century. The causeway appears to have been a pile trestle which was constructed in the first half of the nineteenth century. It was destroyed by a storm after standing a few years. During the latter half of the eighteenth century there was a ferry at the site of the isthmus, which was probably used by Lord Cornwallis for crossing his army to the island while on his way south in July, 1781. About this time he worsted "the boy" Lafayette in a spirited skirmish on the mainland between Green Spring and the island and came here near capturing him.

In constructing the chart of the town and its environs, the localities where a number of historic scenes were enacted were fixed, also the locations, with greater or less exactness, of the grounds or dwellings of a number of the former residents, the sites of two of the town's three forts and of several of its public buildings.

There being no definite information available for determining the positions of the western bank of the head of the island during the Jamestown period, of the original paled town, also of the first fort and early graveyard, it was necessary to depend on reasonable conjecture. On account of not being based on data of a definite character, as are most of the other localities treated of, this part of the investigation is offered with a measure of diffidence. The deductions, however, are believed to be warranted by the evidence. Unfortunately, there is nothing to show who owned the land around the church tower anterior to 1683, where, according to this investigation, before the "New Towne" was established, the earliest town was situated.

The positions of the third and fourth state houses, and the grounds of several persons conspicuous in the affairs of the colony towards the close of the town's career are, however, fixed in and near this older quarter of the town.

A description of the town would be incomplete without some reference to its most interesting feature, the first Anglican church in America. Brief descriptions of the several church structures of " James Citty " parish, erected at " James Citty," are therefore included.

As the page of the Virginia Land Patent Records containing transcripts of two of the earliest patents, viz: to Sir George Yeardley, Knight, and Captain Roger Smith, are missing, it was necessary, for locating the tracts they represented, to depend on the meager information contained in the Patent Record Index, and the renditions of the missing transcripts as contained in the writings of other investigators, which are not very satisfactory.

An appendix comprises the details, in as comprehensive form as possible, of the method of establishing the position of " the New Towne." The plats of several grants which have been located in " the New Towne " are omitted from the " Map of Iames Citty," as by introducing them those of greater antiquity and interest would be covered, and confusion created in the different lines. The parts of some of the plats which extend beyond the limits of the town are also omitted.

All dates are given according to Old Style.

The occasion seems opportune for informing the reader that the credit of rescuing from oblivion and preserving some of the most important ancient landmarks of Virginia, including Jamestown, is entirely due to the Association for the Preservation of Virginia Antiquities. Organized and administered by ladies of the " Old Dominion," the association is not only arousing an ever-increasing interest in events of colonial days, which engenders a spirit of true patriotism, but in spite of a slender exchequer, is achieving remarkable results in preserving historic landmarks.

After exhausting all available sources of information about the town, it is found that a great deal is lacking to make a knowl-

edge of the subject complete and satisfactory. This much, however, is learned, that the town, even though measured by what
would appear to be a standard of its time, was small, poor and
insignificant. This fact invests the place with the deepest interest, when it is remembered that from such a small beginning in
the wilderness has sprung what bids fair to become, if not so
already, the greatest nation of the earth.

Three centuries have elapsed since the laying of the corner-
stone of the nation's foundation. How striking the contrast
between then and now, in the mode of living, in the knowledge
of the sciences and the liberal arts, and in the supersedure of
intolerance and blind superstition by freedom of conscience and
enlightenment !

INDEX TO

"MAP OF JAMES CITTY, VA., 1607-1698."

A—First Ridge, " Block House Hill," belonging to John Bauldwin in 1656.

B—Second ridge, containing tracts of Richard James, John
Bauldwin, Rev. Thomas Hampton, *et al.*

C—Third ridge, on which stood the third and fourth state houses.

D—Fourth ridge, on which the town was principally situated.

a, a, a, a—Jetties constructed in 1895-96 to protect island bank.

1—Approximate position of western shore line of island, 1600-
1700.

2—Present shore line of mainland above the island.

3—Bridge across Back River on road to Williamsburg.

4—Lot of Philip Ludwell, Esq., in 1694, containing the ruins
of three brick houses.

5—Third and fourth state houses, 1666 to 1698.

6—" Country House," in 1694.

7—Part of foundations of building reputed to have been a
powder magazine.

8—Site of brick fort constructed between 1670 and 1676.

9—The lone cypress.

10—Approximate position of northerly line between Richard
James and John Bauldwin in 1657.

11—Approximate site of tract of Richard Saunders, 1644.

12—Approximate site of tract of Edward Challis, 1643.

13—Approximate site of tract of Radulph Spraggon, 1644.

14—Approximate site of tract of Geo. Gilbert, 1643.

15—Probable outline of original paled four-acre town, shown
by red lines.

16—Tract of Edward Chilton, Attorney-General, 1683.

17—Tract of Wm. Edwards, Sr., 1690.

18—Piles of former bridge between island and mainland, constructed during first half of nineteenth century

19—Tract of John Howard, 1694.

20—Tract of Nathaniel Bacon, Sr., 1694. Contains foundation of chimney.

21—Confederate fort constructed in 1861.

22—Ancient tower ruin, inclosed part of old graveyard, and foundation of third, fourth and fifth churches.

23—Probable site of triangular fort constructed in 1607, designated in 18th century MS, "Fort Hill."

24—Probable site of "bridge" (wharf), constructed by Dale in 1611.

25—Probable landing place of first settlers, May 14, 1607, indicated by red flags.

26—Approximate site of blockhouse, built by Captain Richard Stephens in 1624, and probable site of Berkeley's trench.

27—Confederate redoubt commanding Back River, constructed in 1861.

28—Modern ditch draining "Pitch and Tarr Swamp."

29—Boundary lines of tract belonging to the Association for the Preservation of Virginia Antiquities.

30—"The old state house" (approximate), used from about 1630 to 1656, on one-acre tract, of which part was sold to Ludwell and Stegg in 1667. Most probably contained Gov. Harvey's residence prior to 1641, Gov. Berkeley's residence prior to 1656 and subsequently Gov. Bennett's residence.

31—Ruins of building on site of Ambler-Jaquelin messuage.

32—Tract of John Chew, 1624.

33—Tract of Captain Richard Stephens, 1623.

34—Tract of Captain Ralph Hamor, 1624, Secretary of State and chronicler.

35—Site of the turf fort, erected probably about 1663.

36—Cross streets connecting "the way along the Maine River" and the Back Street.

37—Tract of George Menefy, 1624, member of the Council of State.

38—The "way along the Greate river," or "Maine river."

39—Cart track "leading to Island House," in 1665.

40—Causeway over swamp formerly connecting part of island containing "the new towne" with the second ridge.

41—One-acre tract bought by William Sherwood in 1681, "on which formerly stood the brick house formerly called the Country House," and later, probably Sherwood's residence.

42—Jamestown Island wharf.

43—Probable site of tract of Richard Clarke, 1646.

44—The "main cart path."

45—"The old Greate Road," in 1694.

46—Ancient graveyard.

47—Point where skeletons were exposed by bank abrasion in 1895.

48—Shore line of 1903.

49—Traces of house foundations. Probable site of Richard Lawrence's dwelling about 1676.

N. B. Broken lines on map indicate approximate boundaries, etc.

DESCRIPTION OF JAMESTOWN ISLAND.

AMESTOWN Island is situated in James River, sixty-eight and three-fourths miles below the head of tidewater, at the foot of the Richmond rapids, and fifty-eight miles above the Virginia capes.

No ancient charts of the island and town of the Jamestown period (1607-1698), have been discovered. "The Draughte by Roberte Tindall, of Virginia, Anno 1608," and "Chart of Virginia," sent to Philip III of Spain in the same year by Zuñiga to accompany the report of Francisco Maguel,[1] "the Irishman," a spy in the service of Spain, and published in *The Genesis of the United States,* although possessing some merit as reconnoisance sketches, prove to be inaccurate on comparison with modern maps, and furnish information of but little value as to the shape of the island and the site of the town.

The island, thus invariably designated in the old land patents, and so referred to in Ralph Hamor's *Discourse,* and other ancient writings, is two and three-fourths miles long, with a width varying from about three hundred yards at its head to about one and one-fourth miles near its lower extremity. It was formerly connected at its upper extremity with the mainland by a narrow neck, which being at a much lower elevation than the island, constituted an isthmus only at ordinary tides. What appear to be traces of the isthmus are found at one to two feet below low tide, just west of the piling of an old trestle bridge, which formerly connected the island with the mainland. The bridge was destroyed by a storm over fifty years ago. As compared with the neighboring mainland, the general elevation of the island is low.

Adjoining the head of the island is a marsh, which is referred to in the old land patents as "belonging to the Back river."

The head of the island is composed of three ridges and part

---

[1] His name was probably Francis McGill.

of a fourth, marked on accompanying map A, B, C, D, having an easterly trend, and rising to about twelve to sixteen feet above low tide. Between the three uppermost ridges are narrow marshes or slashes. The slash between the first and second formerly connected with Back River only, but by the abrasion of the western shore of the island it would now connect James River with the Back River were it not for the recently constructed sea wall. Between the second and third ridges is a slash or branch of a large swamp situated near the middle of the island and extending easterly to the Back River. It drains into Spratley's Bay, and was anciently referred to as "the Pitch and Tarr Swamp." (See Map, Sketch of Iames Citty Island.) About two hundred yards inland from the western shore of the island the above slash becomes the boundary between the second and fourth ridges.

The boundary between the third and fourth ridges is "a little vale," which, near the river bank, is two to three feet above high tide. This valley, as will appear later, contained near its former river end a brick fort constructed towards the close of the seventeenth century. The head of the fourth ridge is referred to in an eighteenth century MS. as Fort Hill. Here the ground rises quite rapidly to an elevation of about ten feet, and for two small areas to fourteen feet above low tide, forming two knolls, one at the tower ruin and the other in the Confederate fort of 1861. The two knolls were probably "the two Mountaines," on which Percy informs us, in his *Discourse,* "was sowne most of our Corne." The western extremities of the above ridges, as is shown below, prior to the last two centuries extended four or·five hundred feet beyond the present island bank.

Below the fourth ridge is a narrow slash, now partly filled with sand, another branch of the main swamp, in which there is a minute stream referred to in the ancient patents as "Orchard Run," draining the swamp into the river (see sketch of "Iames Citty Island"). East of the last mentioned slash is a ridge, also having an easterly trend. East of the above ridge and extending to James River is a branch of a great marsh, referred to below. Next follows a series of seven low ridges, forming collectively what was anciently known as Goose Hill. The Goose Hill ridges are separated by slashes of the extensive marsh above referred to, lying north and east of them, named Goose Hill marsh. It is drained into James River by Passmore's or Paschmore's Creek.

Goose Hill is a hill only in the same relative sense that the two knolls where the English wheat was planted were mountains. The fourth ridge has a larger area of good soil above extreme high tide than the other ridges at the head of the island. The Back River, which is referred to in many of the old patents, forms the northern boundary of the island. Although its channel is from seven to twenty-three feet deep, the depth on the bar in Spratley's Bay, into which it empties, is but four feet; ample, however, for the crossing of the "friggett," from which the landing in Back River near the head of the island was named, and of whose coming the town's people were apprised by a musical note, as the vessel rounded "Pyping Point," [2]

Above the Back River was situated "Sandy Bay," having the isthmus for its western and "Powhatan Swamp" for its eastern boundary, and receiving on the north the flow of Powhatan Creek. Near the northeastern shore of the bay, about a mile from "James Towne," was situated what is believed to have been the first American glass works, in which beads were manufactured for trading with the Indians.

As will appear later, the two branches of "Pitch and Tarr Swamp" above mentioned were the upper and lower limits of the principal part of "James Citty." A line of stumps, visible at low tide, extending shoreward from a solitary cypress standing two hundred and seventy feet from the recently constructed sea wall, probably indicates the former position of the head of the upper branch of the swamp, where, as will be shown further on, a tract of land was granted in 1696 to Lieutenant Edward Ross.

---

[2] The point was located by platting a patent to Richard James (Virginia Land Patent Records, Book III, p. 368).

The mean tidal range at Jamestown Island is but twenty-two inches. Great tides, however, rising to seven or eight feet above low water, are occasionally caused by gales from between south and east. Whenever the tide rose slightly above its normal level, the isthmus was submerged. During great tides there is a flow from the river through the depression between the third and fourth ridges into the upper branch of the swamp.[3]

---

[3] By the extension of the sea wall in 1905 and 1906, this flow is prevented.

THE SEA WALL
From Block House Hill

ABRASION OF THE ISLAND.

NTIL 1901, the length of the western bank exposed to abrasion was about a half mile. In the above year about half of the exposed bank was protected by the sea wall before mentioned. This part of the wall ended at the third ridge, thus fortunately protecting from the encroachments of the river the ground which two years later was found to contain the old state house foundations. The shore of the mainland from a short distance above the island to the Chickahominy River, a distance of about six miles, is being abraded, and there are unmistakable signs of this action being operative for a very long period in the past. There is very good evidence that this bank was being abraded by the waves as early as 1686. The above shore, on account of its projection, originally formed a natural protection for the island headland, and by its recession the latter became exposed to wave action.

It would hardly seem possible that the abrasion of the island was in progress as early as 1686, or even in 1696, as in the latter year a grant of land, situated on its western bank, contiguous to and below the upper branch of " Pitch and Tarr Swamp " was made to Lieutenant Edward Ross,[1] before alluded to. It seems probable that the island was not attacked by the river before 1700. Under this assumption, therefore, the whole period of the island's abrasion to the time of its protection in 1901, would be two hundred and one years. Observation of the bank in recent years shows that its annual rate of recession has been about four feet. Prior to the extensive use of side wheel steamers on James River, probably about 1860, and when occasional strong winds between west and north were the sole destroying agents, the rate probably did not exceed two feet. Applying the above rates for forty years and one hundred and

[1] Virginia Land Patent Records, Book IX, p. 49.

sixty-one years respectively, the total width of the prism of abrasion would amount to about 482 feet.

From the data contained in the following quotation from *Amoenitates Graphicae,* a magazine edited by Professor Louis Hue Girardin, in 1803,[2] "many yards of the palisades erected by the first settlers are yet to be seen at a low tide standing at least 150 to 200 paces from the present shore," it would appear that the annual rate of abrasion, assuming the pace at thirty inches, was about twice that given above. Professor Girardin's description, however, shows that he was not accustomed to estimating distances, and his figures, therefore, do not appear to have any value.

As the time when the abrasion began and its rate from time to time are unknown, no reliable deduction can be made as to the exact position of the western shore of the island in the seventeenth century.

From the Edward Ross patent, the direction of the shore for two hundred and fifteen feet, immediately below the head of the upper branch of "Pitch and Tarr Swamp," is learned to have then been about S. 3° W. (corrected for declination) or about the same as that of the present western shore at the third ridge.

In 1891 there still remained, about sixty yards above the Confederate fort, the lower part of the island headland, projecting about thirty yards from the general line of the shore and forming a sharp point, modernly known as "Church Point." The lower side of the point in the above year furnishes the general direction of the southern shore of the headland.

In the account of the bi-centenary celebration at Jamestown Island in 1807, it is stated that the "Lady Washington," one of the visiting vessels, anchored "in a beautiful cove in the form of a crescent, which stretching on either side afforded a safe and expanded bason."[3]

---

[2] Foot note, page 8, *Report of the Proceedings of the Late Jubilee at James-Town* (in 1807).

[3] *Report of the Proceedings of the Late Jubilee at James-Town,* p. 7.

The point above mentioned, then projecting several hundred feet further westward than the present shore, undoubtedly formed the head of the cove. Its foot was about five-eighths of a mile below its head, and is marked by an old abandoned wharf which was in use in 1861. The shore of the cove below the new wharf remains about as it was when the island was first settled.

The description of a course in the survey notes of a patent to William Sherwood[4] "and by the same [Back River] to Sandy Bay, to a persimmon tree under Block House Hill, *thence under the said hill six chains to James River,*" shows that the head of the island at the southern end of the isthmus was about 200 feet wide.

From patents issued to Alexander Stonar in 1637, and to Richard Sanders in 1644, for land situated on the first ridge; to Edward Challis in 1643, to Radulph Spraggon in 1644, and to John Bauldwin in 1656,[5] on the second ridge, it would appear that the general direction of the western bank of the island at its upper extremity was approximately the same as it is to-day. On account of incomplete descriptions, the true positions of the above tracts cannot be determined. As even their approximate locations give them some value, they are shown on the map. From a reference in the Spraggon patent the approximate position of part of "the way leading towards the mayne," near the head of the island, is established.

From the preceding data the shape of the head of the island during the "James Citty" period, as exhibited on the map, was determined.

Since the first settlement of the island by the English, probably twenty acres at its western extremity have been lost by abrasion. The abraded area comprises principally parts of the uppermost three ridges, and a very small proportion of the fourth ridge. The tidal currents at Jamestown are too light to erode the clay of which the banks at the head of the island are

---

[4] Va. Land Pat. Records, Book VII, p. 384, *et seq.*

[5] Va. Land Pat. Records, Book I, p. 466; Book II, pp. 11, 12; Book IV, p. 88.

formed. Wave action developed in the long reach of wide water extending in a northwesterly direction has been the destroying agent, the waves from every passing steam vessel contributing to the work of destruction.

From the observation of the height of waves at Jamestown Island, it seems evident that their abrading effect does not reach to greater depths than three or four feet below low water. The one fathom curve on the map, therefore, is considerably west of the extreme outer limits of the western shore line during the "James Citty" period.

Landing Place

of the First Settlers.

THE trough of the channel off the head of the island has steep sides, and is from fifty to ninety feet deep. As it lies in a bed of dense, tough clay, the scouring effect of the light currents of the locality, continuing even for centuries, should be very slight. From the deposition of material worn from the island and the shore above, there has probably been a slight diminution of depth during the past three hundred years in the thalweg or deepest part of the channel, but little or none on its sides. The above remark is intended to apply particularly to the vicinity of Jamestown Island. At other localities on James River battures have formed under projecting points between the trough of the channel and the shores.

The hydrographic contours off the western shore of the island show the channel gradually nearing that shore from above until it approaches to within about one hundred and seventy-five yards of it, at about three hundred yards above the tower ruin (see contours on map). Below the ruin it gradually leaves the island and opposite the former site of the turf fort, hereinafter referred to, is about three hundred and fifty yards from the shore. The contours also exhibit a stretch of channel upwards of two hundred and fifty feet long at the point of divergence above the tower ruin, having its north side steeper than elsewhere in the above reach of river.

According to the rate of abrasion above determined the western shore of the island extended to the part of the channel having the steep sides during the seventeenth century.

According to Master George Percy's *Discourse*, the ships, at the first landing place of the settlers, were moored to trees standing on the river bank, contiguous to which the water depth was six fathoms. The modern contours of the channel, as has been pointed out, cannot differ materially from those existing when the first settlement was made. The part of the side of the channel, therefore, which is steepest, and to which the island bank formerly extended, is manifestly the spot where the settlers debarked May 14, 1607, and of which Percy wrote, "where our shippes doe lie so neere the shoare that they are moored to the Trees in six fathom water."

The landing was well selected for convenience of discharging the ship's cargoes and very few similarly suitable exist on James River. As Archer's Hope, on the mainland opposite the lower end of the island, was regarded as a very desirable location for the first settlement, and was rejected only on account of its shore being made inaccessible to Newport's vessels by shallow water the day before the island was selected, it is apparent that the ease of discharging the vessels' cargoes directly on the river bank outweighed many other far more important considerations in deciding on the abiding place of the settlers.

LOCATION OF FIRST FORT AND TOWN.

HE first fort, "which was triangle wise, having three Bulwarkes at every corner like a halfe Moone and foure or five pieces of Artillerie mounted in them," was completed June 15—the 31st day after the first settlers disembarked.[1] As there is no information extant as to the site of the first fort, that detail will have to be arrived at inductively. It was not at the original landing place, for, from the letter of Sir Thomas Dale, of May 25, 1611,[2] " to the President and Counsell of the Companie of Adventurers and Planters in Virginia," it is learned that immediately after his arrival at James Towne to succeed Lord La Warr as deputy governor, " a bridge to land our goods safe and dry upon," *i. e.,* a wharf, was constructed by Captain Newport and "his Mariners." The construction of this wharf is alluded to in the " Breife Declaration,"[3] as follows:

"A framed Bridge was alsoe then erected, [during Sir Thomas Smith's administration] which utterly decayed before the end of Sir Thomas Smith's government, that being the only bridge (any way soe to be called) that was ever in the country."

From the above it is obvious that the water was too shallow for vessels to lie against the shore in front of the fort, which, therefore, as above stated, was not at the original landing-place. It was, however, probably not far distant, for if otherwise, the settlers, with their limited means of carriage, would have been at great labor in moving their equipment, stores and ordnance. A natural site for the fort would have been just east of the " little vale " at the upper extremity of the fourth ridge. Thus situated, the guns of its north bastion would have swept the

---

[1] Percy's *Discourse.*

[2] *The Genesis of the United States, p.* 488.

[3] A Breife Declaration of the Plantation of Virginia, &c., *McDonald Papers,* Vol. I, pp. 103-142.

branch of the swamp below and of the vale above, while those of its east and west bastions would have commanded the river front and the channel approaching from below, as did the guns of its successor, the Confederate fort of 1861. In the above described position the part of the branch of the swamp between the second and fourth ridges would have afforded additional protection against the Indians. The third ridge was possibly strategically as favorable as the fourth, but its crest is two feet lower and its area above the level of great tides much smaller. It was, therefore, not as well adapted to the needs of the first settlers.

In excavating earth in 1861, at the head of the fourth ridge near the Confederate fort for its construction, pieces of armor and weapons of the early " James Towne " period were found, a good indication that the fort of 1607 was located about as above described. From the shore in front of it a wharf only about two hundred feet long would have been required to reach water twelve feet deep.

The parade ground where " the whole Company every Saturday exercised, in the plaine by the west Bulwarke, prepared for that purpose " * * * " where sometimes more than an hundred Salvages would stand in an amazement to behold, how a fyle would batter a tree, where he [Captain John Smith] would make them a marke to shoot at," * was on the plateau at the head of the fourth ridge between the western curtain of the triangular fort and the " little vale." As shown on the map, it was three hundred feet long and upwards of one hundred feet wide.

From the " Breife Declaration," it is learned that " After this first supplie " [January, 1608], " there were some few poore howses built, & entrance made in cleeringe of grounde to the quantitye of foure acres for the whole Collony, hunger & sickness not permittinge any great matters to be donne that yeare." It does not seem probable that the clearing, on account of its small area, was made for agricultural purposes, for while Captain

---

* Works, Captain John Smith, p. 433.

John Smith was president, probably in the spring of 1609, or about a year after the clearing of the four acres was begun, thirty or forty acres of ground were worked and planted.[5] Whatever may have been the purpose for which the four-acre tract was intended, it is evident from what follows that it, or some other tract of the same area, was subsequently surrounded by a stockade and formed the town.

Further on in the same narrative by the "ancient planters" appears the following: "Fortification against a foreign enemy there was none, only two or three peeces of ordinance mounted, & against a domestic [enemy] noe other but a pale inclosinge the Towne, to the quantitye of foure acres within which those buildings that weare erected, could not in any man's judgement, neither did stand above five yeares & that not without continuall reparations."

The part of the "Declaration" from which the above is extracted is ambiguous and obscure, the settlements at Henrico near Dutch Gap, about 14 miles below Richmond, and James Towne being described, as it were, in the same breath. It would appear, however, from the context that the four acres were at the latter place, and this view is indirectly confirmed by Ralph Hamor, who, as appears from the following, gives the area of Henrico as seven acres; "and in the beginning of September, 1611, he [Dale] set from Iamestown, and in a day & a halfe, landed at a place where he purposed to seate & builde, where he had not bin ten daies before he had very strongly impaled seuen English Acres of ground for a towne."[6]

There are no data available giving the slightest clue as to the situation of the four acres. It is believed that they included the area of one acre covered by the first fort, as it is quite improbable that the settlers had two distinct towns at the same place.

Shortly after Captain John Smith became president of the

---

[5] *Ibid*, pp. 154, 471.

[6] *A True Discourse of the present estate of Virginia*, p. 29.

colony (September, 1608) the plan of the fort was reduced to "a five-square form." [7] This is construed to apply to the form of the town, after it was enlarged as noted above.

The safest and, therefore, the most natural position for the three-acre addition, would have been adjoining the eastern bulwark of the triangular fort. From its southern end the miniature town, fronting the river, probably extended east about one hundred yards, thence in a northerly direction to and along the eastern wall of the graveyard, thence northwesterly by "the old Greate Roade" given as the eastern boundary of a tract granted John Howard in 1694,[8] and thence westerly by a line which subsequently formed the southern boundary of Richard Lawrence's tract, and in the line of its prolongation about at the level of great tides—eight feet above low water—to the north bastion of the triangular fort, whose western and southern bulwarks completed the inclosure. These lines would make the fort "a five-square form" or pentagon. "The old Greate Road," judging from its name, was of great antiquity. It was probably one of the first roads opened by the settlers, and passed along one of the paled sides of the early town, as above described.

The original triangular fort must have been maintained for several years as an inner stronghold of the paled town. During Strachey's sojourn in the colony, from May, 1610, to the fall of 1611, the principal buildings were situated within it. The stockade around the part of the town outside of the fort proper was probably kept up for some time after the massacre of 1622, until the settlement gained a sufficient foothold to make it unnecessary as a defence against the Indians.

The greater part of the ground inclosed by the triangular fort has been destroyed by the abrasion of the island bank.

---

[7] Works, Captain John Smith, p. 433.
[8] Va. Land Patent Records, Book VIII, p. 82.

Locations of Block Houses.

FOR preventing incursions of the Indians across the isthmus, Captain John Smith, in the spring of 1609, "built a Blockhouse in the neck of our Isle." This was replaced by a similar structure about 1624. The latter is referred to in a patent to John Bauldwin in 1656, which locates it approximately. It appears, from the patent, that the later block house was near the earlier one. The ridge on which the block houses were placed, the first ridge, is referred to in the patents as Block House Hill. A "bank of earth not a flight shot long cast up thwart the neck of the peninsula" by Sir William Berkeley, in September, 1676, to oppose the entrance of Bacon's men to "James Citty"[1] must have been situated on the north side of Block House Hill at the southern end of the isthmus.

There were also, according to Ralph Hamor, two block houses "to observe and watch least the Indians at any time should swim over the back river and come into the Island." He does not, however, give their locations. They were on the Back River, one probably at Friggett Landing, the other below Governor Yeardley's place.

---

[1] The Beginning, Progress and Conclusion of Bacon's Rebellion in Virginia in the years 1675 and 1676, by T. M.—*Force's Historical Tracts*, Vol. I, p. 21.

DESCRIPTION OF THE TOWN.

HE cluster of huts constituting the habitations of the first hundred settlers, enfolded in its chrysalis-like stockade, was hardly entitled to the appellation of town. The term city, given the collection of unpretentious brick buildings of a later day, was equally a misnomer.

For the details of the first structures erected, as of most other matters pertaining to the early settlement, Captain John Smith is the principal authority.

As the time of Newport's colony, immediately after its arrival in Virginia was occupied in exploring the country, building the stockade, and preparing a cargo for the return voyage of the ships, the building of quarters was neglected, and those erected were inadequate in number and afforded but imperfect shelter. The best of them were built of rails and roofed with marsh grass thatch covered with earth.[1] According to the "Breife Declaration," some of the settlers lived in holes in the ground, as is sometimes done on the western plains, where they are called "dug-outs."

After Newport's departure, hot weather and general illness of the party supervening, the completing of the huts was prevented until the fall of 1607.[2]

The first huts were destroyed by fire in January, 1608, and were not fully replaced until after Newport's departure for England, in April of that year,[3] about which time the clearing of the four acres was begun.

The huts which replaced those that were burned were more comfortable than the latter. Their sides were lined with Indian

[1] Works, Captain John Smith, p. 957. (The references in this monograph to "Works, Captain John Smith," are from Prof. Edward Arber's edition.)
[2] *Ibid*, pp. 10, 96, 392.   [3] *Ibid*, pp. 105, 409.

mats, and the roofs made of boards.[4] They were apparently without floors. Improvements were gradually made in hut construction by roofing with the bark of trees so as to shed water, probably in the same manner as half cylinder roofing tiles are used, and erecting "wide and large country chimneys," of wattles plastered with clay.[5] About a year later twenty additional houses were added,[5] and, when Captain Smith left the settlement in 1609, it had, according to his account, within the fort, then equipped with twenty-four guns of different calibers, of which, however, probably not over six were mounted in the bastions, besides the church and store house, forty or fifty of the above huts.[7] Dr. Simmonds states that there were fifty or sixty houses within the stockade,[8] where also was situated the well, prior to digging which the settlers drank the often brackish water of the river. The well water, naturally enough, was filled with organic matter. It undoubtedly caused most of the malaria and enteric troubles of the settlers. It was found to be in an unsanitary condition by Dale in 1611, resulting probably from its proximity to the huts. Dale proposed, among other improvements to be made in the town, the digging of a new well. In 1617 the new well was found to be polluted.[9]

The fort undoubtedly stood above the level of great tides, as otherwise, Captain John Smith or others would have referred in their writings to the discomforts arising from tidal inundations. Judging from the contours of the ground, at or adjoining the site of the fort, its elevation was not less than seven or eight feet above low water.[10]

---

[4] *Ibid*, pp. 502, 503.   [5] *Purchas His Pilgrimes, Lib.* IX, p. 1752.
[6] Works, Captain John Smith. pp. 154, 471.
[7] *Ibid*, p. 612.   [8] *Ibid*, p. 486.
[9] Works, Captain John Smith, p. 535.
[10] The depth of the well in the fort is given by Strachey in *Purchas His Pilgrimes* at six or seven fathoms. This, evidently, is a misprint, and should read six or seven feet. The level of the water in wells on the island follows that of the tides. The bottom of an ancient well on the third ridge is about 1½ feet below low tide. A proper depth for a well in the fort would probably have been 7 to 9½ feet, depending on the elevation of the ground.

According to Strachey, whose writings show that he was well grounded in the humanities, although not so well versed in the science of numbers, the ground enclosed by the first fort had an area of a half-acre. The fort was a stockade about fourteen feet high, formed of trees set about four feet in the ground. Its south curtain or bulwark was one hundred and forty yards long and the other two sides one hundred yards each. It is inferred from each of the pales forming a load for two or three men, that they were eight to ten inches in diameter.[11]

It is very improbable that the fort had any earthworks. It had three entrances or ports, one through each curtain or bulwark, the principal one being through the south curtain. Within the stockade, facing each port, was a fieldpiece.

The huts were arranged in rows parallel to the curtains with a street thirty to thirty-six feet wide intervening. Within the hollow triangle formed by the lines of huts, and having probably an area of about a half acre, were the guard house, the market place and the chapel " in length three score foote in breadth twenty-foure." [12]

Dr. Simmonds gives the width of the streets between the lines of huts and the palisades at eight to ten yards.[13]

In 1611, Sir Thomas Dale erected a "munition-house," a powder-house, a fish-house, a shelter-shed for cattle and a stable,[14] and a few months later Sir Thomas Gates added a storehouse, covering a space of one hundred and twenty by forty feet and a number (not given) of log houses arranged in two rows, some of which were two stories and a garret high. About this time also the stockade was repaired and a new gun platform placed at its western end, presumably at the point of the triangular fort known as the west bastion.[15] It is apparent that if all of the

[11] Works, Captain John Smith, p. 612.

[12] Purchas His Pilgrimes, Liber IX, pp. 1752, 1753.

[13] Works, Captain John Smith, p. 407.

[14] The Genesis of the United States. p. 492.

[15] Hamor's True Discourse, p. 33.

different structures above enumerated were situated within the triangular fort, whose area was a small fraction more than one acre, there would have remained little or no room for the three or four hundred people who sometimes constituted the population. Some of the buildings, therefore, were outside of the triangle and in other parts of the paled town. The place must now have presented an appearance similar to that of some of our earlier frontier posts.

On account, no doubt, of unseasoned or sappy timber being used for the log houses, but five or six remained serviceable in 1617.[16] No improvements, however, appear to have been made after Gates' second administration in 1614, or new buildings added except the wooden church last referred to, whose dimensions were fifty by twenty feet, until Sir George Yeardley's arrival in 1619.

In 1623 there were but twenty-two dwellings at "James Citty," a seemingly insufficient number to accommodate the new settlers who, on their way to the interior, for several years, had been arriving in large numbers. The massacre of 1622 and unfavorable reports of the colony published by several unprincipled partisans of Sir Thomas Smythe, treasurer or governor of the London Company, to create prejudice against and destroy confidence in the Virginia enterprise under the administrations of Sir Edwin Sandys, Smythe's successor, and of the Earl of Southampton, who succeeded Sandys, checked the growth of the colony and, to some extent, therefore, that of the town.

For many years the place apparently made little or no progress. On February 20, 1636, a law was enacted by the Grand Assembly[17] providing for a grant of a house lot and garden plot to every settler that would build thereon within six months. A similar law was made in 1638, and, as a result, twelve dwellings and stores, including the first brick house of the colony, sixteen

---

[16] Works, Captain John Smith, p. 535.
[17] Virginia Land Patent Records, Book I, p. 689.

by twenty-four feet in plan, were erected. Within the year following all the lots along the town's water front were patented.[18]

The patent records contain eight land grants made within the
town precincts between 1636 and 1642.[19] In the latter year Sir
William Berkeley, the new governor, arrived bearing instructions from the Royal government to rebuild the town with brick
houses. According to the instructions every person who, " within a convenient time," should erect in any town of the colony a
brick dwelling sixteen by twenty-four feet with a cellar would be
granted five hundred acres of land. The colonial government
was also empowered, in view of the existing town having proved
unhealthy, to build a new one elsewhere, which, however, should
bear the original name of " James Towne."[20] In March, 1643,
the Grand Assembly framed a statute, according to which
builders of houses on deserted lots in " James Citty " would
acquire a title to the lot built on, provided the back quit rents
were paid.[21]

The patent transcripts contain twelve issues for town lots between 1642 and 1662. At the close of the interregnum in 1661,
during Sir William Berkeley's second term as governor of Virginia, he was again urged by the king to take steps to enlarge
the town by erecting more houses, the monarch assuring him
that " Wee will take it very well at their hands if they [the
members of the colonial council] will each of them build one or
more houses there."[22]

In deference to the king's wish, an act was passed at the next
ensuing session of the Assembly, inhibiting the building of any
more wooden houses, and prescribing that there should be

---

[18] *McDonald Papers*, Vol. I, pp. 247-249. Governor Harvey and
Council to Privy Council, January, 1639.

[19] Virginia Land Patent Records, Book I, pp. 466, 587, 588, 595,
598, 689, 730. Reference is made hereinafter to the incompleteness
of the records.

[20] Instructions to Governor Berkeley and Council, August, 1641.—
McDonald Papers, Vol. I, p. 383.

[21] *Hening's Statutes*, Vol. I, p. 252.

[22] Instructions to Governor Berkeley, *McDonald Papers*, Vol. I, p. 414.

erected at "James Citty" thirty-two brick houses, forty by twenty feet in plan inside, apparently two stories high, and roofed with slate or tile.[23] Each of the seventeen counties was required to build, at its expense, one of the houses. The above attempt to force the town's growth was a failure, for in 1676, at the outbreak of Bacon's Rebellion, the community held but sixteen or eighteen dwellings, most "as is the church built of brick, faire and large; and in them a dozen families (for all the houses are not inhabited) getting their liveings by keeping of ordinaries at extreordinary rates."[24] The unoccupied houses were some of those which had been ordered built by statute of December, 1662, but had never been completed,[25] most probably on account of the poverty of their builders.

In 1676 the entire town was destroyed by Bacon as a strategic measure.

In 1682, Lord Culpeper, the governor, received instructions from England to rebuild, the royal good will being again tendered, as in the message to Berkeley of 1661, to the members of the council and prominent citizens of the town who should initiate the work. Two good houses had at that time been erected by Colonel Bacon the elder, and others were either under construction or proposed. Lord Culpeper's reply to the king's message contains a reason for the town's lack of recuperative power. "I have given all encouragement possible for the rebuilding of James Citty, The Generall Courts, publick offices, and meetings of Assemblies having been always kept there, And Greenspring (the nearest convenient habitation) My place of Residence. But there being an Apprehension in many persons that there are other places in the Country more proper for a Metropolis, And that the aforesaid Act for Building Townes, would make one in the most naturall place, there hath not till now of late been Any Great Advance therein. As to the proposall of Building Houses

[23] *Hening's Statutes*, Vol II, p. 172.

[24] Burwell MS., *Force's Historical Tracts*, Vol. I, *Bacons Proseedings*.

[25] British State Papers, Colonial, No. 62.

by those of the Councell and the cheefe Inhabitants, It hath been once attempted in vaine, nothing but profitt and advantage can doe it, and then there will be noe need of Anything else." [26]

In 1697 the number of houses in the town was reported to be twenty or thirty.

In 1698, the royal mandate to build up the town was reiterated to Governor Nicholson, but before any steps could be taken to act on it, a fire occurred, by which the statehouse and prison,[27] and probably all other buildings on the third ridge, were destroyed.

At a session of the General Assembly held in April, 1699, acts were passed for establishing the city of Williamsburg (about eight miles north-east of "James Towne"), for erecting a statehouse there and providing for raising funds to defray its cost by imposing an import tax on slaves, also on servants not born in England or Wales, brought to the colony.[28]

After the fire of 1698, "James Citty" waned. One patent for a small tract in the town, issued in October, 1699,[29] is of record, but no new houses are known to have been erected. Twenty-three years later, the place comprised nothing but "Abundance of Brick Rubbish and three or four good inhabited Houses, tho' the Parish is of pretty large Extent, but less than others." [30]   In 1807, there were two dwellings on the island, the Jaquelin-Ambler and Travis mansions, and in 1861, but one, the former, which was burned during the ensuing war. The above house was afterwards rebuilt, and again burned in 1896. The ground on which it formerly stood was probably owned by Sir Francis Wyatt in 1623. At some time prior to 1690 it belonged to John Page, clerk of the Assembly, from whom it was purchased by William Sherwood.[31]

---

[26] *McDonald Papers*, Vol. VI, p. 165.

[27] *The Present State of Virginia*, by Hugh Jones, A. M., p. 25.

[28] *Hening's Statues*, Vol. III, pp. 193 and 197.

[29] Va. Land Pat. Records, Book IX, p. 232.

[30] *The Present State of Virginia*, by Hugh Jones, A. M., p. 25.

[31] Va. Land Pat. Records, Book VIII, p. 384.

POPULATION OF THE TOWN AND COLONY.

DURING the first eighteen years of the settling of Virginia there were great fluctuations in the population of the colony, and also of "James Forte" or "James Towne." Each influx of new life was followed by a more or less rapid ebbing of the human tide, resulting from the ravages of disease and the tomahawk. During the first eight months the fort's population dwindled from one hundred and five to a little band of thirty-eight persons, the smallest number that the colony ever held. By the arrival of several reinforcements during the twenty-one months following (January, 1608, to October, 1609), its population was increased to upwards of 490.[1] Within eight months the above number was reduced by death from starvation, climatic illness, and pestilence, to about sixty persons. Fresh accessions under Gates and La Warr in June, 1610, brought the number up to about 350, most of whom were quartered in the town. In a few months this number was diminished by death to about 200. Thus far about 900 persons had been sent from England to Virginia, of whom about 700 had perished. The numbers and mortality of Virginia emigrants for the ensuing twenty years as given by different authorities are discrepant.

Between December, 1606, and November, 1619, it is estimated that 2,540 persons emigrated to Virginia, of whom 1,640 died.[2] Between the latter date and February, 1625, 4,749 colonists came to Virginia and 4,400 died, thus making a total mortality in about nineteen years of 6,040, out of 7,289.[3]

According to John Wroth, a member of the Warwick faction, up to 1623, 3,570 out of 5,270 colonists died in the four years

---

[1] Works, Captain John Smith, p. 486. The numbers reported brought by different vessels indicate a less number.

[2] *The First Republic in America*, pp. 285, 329.

[3] *Ibid*, p. 612.

ending with 1622.[4] Captain Nathaniel Butler represented that up to the winter of 1622, the mortality was 8,000 out of 10,000,[5] while the resident colonists declared that up to the winter of 1622 not over 6,000 were sent to Virginia, of whom 2,500 were living.[6] Captain John Smith says: "neere 7,000 people" out of 8,500 had died to 1627.[7]

As pointed out above, there were in June, 1610, about 350 people at "James Towne." In 1616, there were on the entire island fifty persons, under Lieutenant Sharpe. It is stated that in the following year there were 400 persons at "James Towne," of whom, on account of sickness, only one-half were effective.[8]

A census taken in 1623 gives the population of the town at 183. It also shows that during the preceding year, eighty-nine had died in the town.[9]

Although "James Citty" had now assumed more of the proportions of a town, it possessed none of the attractions or allurements which would demand expenditures of money, and probably but few opportunities for making it in trade. The simple, primitive tastes of the settlers, coupled with their general poverty, made shops superfluous. In 1625 the town had one merchant's store.[10] An attempt was made in 1649 to hold a bi-weekly market. This was a complete failure and six years later, the act providing for the market was repealed.[11]

Nearly all who came to the colony, except the officials, had all to make and little to spend. The population of the town, therefore, did not keep pace with that of the colony, in which, after about the first twenty-five years, it slowly but steadily in-

---

[4] *The Genesis of the United States,* p. 1064.

[5] *The Unmasked Face.*

[6] *The Denial of Nathaniel Butler's "The Unmasked Face,"* Neill's *History of the Va. Company,* p. 405.

[7] Works, Captain John Smith, p. 884.   [8] *Ibid,* p. 536

[9] McDonald Papers, Vol. I.

[10] *The First Republic in America,* p. 623.

[11] *Hening's Statutes,* Vol. I, pp. 362, 397.

creased. In 1634 it amounted to 5,119;[12] in 1649, to 15,000;[13] in 1665, to 40,000;[14] in 1681, to 70,000 or 80,000;[15] and in 1715 to 95,000.[16] The function of the town was that of furnishing a place for the assembling of the Legislature and for holding courts. Its permanent population, after about 1623, comprised only a part of the bureaucracy of the colony, and tavern keepers, with their respective families, amounting possibly to one hundred persons, which approximate number was periodically doubled by the meetings of the Assembly and court.

---

[12] State Papers, Colonial, Vol. 8, No. 65, 1634, De Jarnette Papers.

[13] Force's *Historical Tracts*, Vol. II. *A Perfect Description of Virginia*, p. 1.

[14] Winder Papers, Vol. I, p. 187.

[15] Sainsbury Abstracts, Vol. 1681-1685, par. 275. Of this number 76 per cent. were freemen.

[16] Chalmer's *American Colonies*, Vol. II, p. 7.

Sufferings of the Early Colonists.

HE settlement near the head of Jamestown Island was at first called " James Forte " and " James Towne," usually the latter. After the town was enlarged in 1608, and until about 1620, or shortly after the close of Sir Thomas Smythe's administration as governor of the London Company, it was almost invariably referred to by the latter appellation.

The sufferings of the colonists during the above period have probably never been surpassed or even equalled in measure or degree in any other pioneer colony. Under the Smythe regime the colonists' greatest sufferings resulted from hunger. Hand in hand with famine stalked pestilence, yellow fever communicated by vessels bound for " James Towne " which had touched at the West Indies, and bubonic plague and cholera brought from London. Fevers and dysentery resulting from exposure, noxious exhalations from the surrounding marshes and from forest mould for the first time exposed to the heat of the summer sun, impure drinking water and the mosquito all had their share in decimating the colony. The medical treatment then in vogue doubtless increased the mortality, bringing fatal results to many who, without it would have recovered. That the leaders did not succumb was no doubt largely due to nearly all being in the prime of manhood and inured to hardship through the campaigns against the Spaniards in the Netherlands, by which experience they had learned how to avert some of the bad effects of camp life.

As the colonists were but meagerly supplied with provisions from England and raised but few food products, their labor being principally employed in producing tobacco and other articles for export, for the benefit of the London Company, their subsistence during the first four or five years was derived principally from the Indian, either by force or barter. They were not permitted to engage in planting on their own account, except on condition of contributing a part of their crops and one month's services annually to the London Company. Their letters to and from England were intercepted and proffers of assistance to the company in behalf of individual colonists from their friends were declined, with the assurance that they were well provided for. None was allowed to leave Virginia, except by special permission, and it is narrated that a passport from the king for the return of a colonist to England was sewed in a garter to insure its delivery.[1]

The settlers were, to all purposes, in a state of servitude, from which, as a special favor, some were offered release on condition of working three years on Fort Charles. The abhorrence with which life in the colony was regarded is exemplified by a statement in a letter from the Spanish Ambassador in London to Philip III, of Spain, in December, 1616, that while two of three thieves under sentence of death availed themselves of the alternative of going to Virginia, the third preferred hanging.[2]

The climax of suffering was reached when on June 7, 1610, the sixty survivors of four hundred and ninety settlers of but eight months before, broken in health and crushed in spirit, turned their backs on the odious town where tragedy had been almost continually enacted for three years. So deeply impressed by the abject misery of this remnant had been the members of the lately arrived party of Sir Thomas Gates that they had readily joined in the flight from suffering and horrors which they believed would be their lot if they tarried at the ill-favored spot. This, the climax of the critical period of the colony, was safely passed when the astute La Warr, newly appointed governor of Virginia, being apprised on his arrival from England at Point Comfort of the intended abandonment of the colony, thwarted the plan by despatching Captain Brewster ahead of his fleet to meet the forlorn party, and turned it back to the deserted post,

---

[1] *A Briefe Declaration*, etc., McDonald Papers, Vol. I, pp. 103-142
[2] *The Genesis of the United States*, p. 900.

where the tragedy was renewed for another and longer term of years.

An amelioration of the colonists' condition was brought about by the election in 1619, of Sir Edwin Sandys, as successor to Sir Thomas Smythe, to the office of treasurer or governor of the London Company. Even before the new administration was elected, the former policy of the company, which had been actuated by commercial avarice, was abandoned, through the influence of the Sandys party, which inaugurated in its stead one inspired by broad and liberal views. The "most severe and cruel" "Lavves, Diuine, Morall and Martiall," were repealed, and courts of justice established after the manner of those of the mother country; the "ancient planters" who had arrived before the time of Dale were released from further service to the colony, land titles were confirmed and the individual ownership of land introduced by patent. The colony was also allowed to elect its own legislative body. The last mentioned privilege, however, although enjoyed in 1619, does not appear to have been officially promulgated until the publication of the written constitution in 1621,[3] under the administration of Sir Henry Wriothesley, Earl of Southampton, who had succeeded Sir Edwin Sandys in 1620. These reforms and privileges stimulated the colony to renewed efforts and led to the development of its principal town.

As late as 1623, however, when the needs of the colonists should have been understood in England, their condition was often deplorable. Statements by members of the crew of one of the ships arriving in Virginia in that year attested to newly arrived emigrants dying in the streets of James Towne, and lying there until the dogs had eaten their bodies. A most forlorn and mournful message from Virginia of this time is a letter of Richard Frethorne, of Martin's Hundred, about seven miles below Jamestown, to his parents in England, that "since he landed he had eaten nothing but pease and loblolly (water gruel). He had seen no venison and was not allowed to go

---

[3] *Hening's Statutes*, Vol. I, pp. 110, 111, 112.

after waterfowl, but had to work both early and late for a mess of water gruel and a mouthful of bread and beef. The people cried out ' Oh ! that they were in England without their limbs * * * though they begged from door to door.' There was nothing to be got but sickness and death, except that one had money to lay out in some things for profit but (I) have nothing at all, no not a shirt to (my) back, but two rags, nor no clothes but one poor suit, nor but one pair of shoes, but one pair of stockings, but one cap, but two bands." His cloak had been stolen by one of his fellows. He had not a penny to help him to " spice " or sugar, or strong waters, without which it was impossible to live. He had grown weak, for he had often eaten more in a day at home tha ι was now allowed him for a week, and his parents had often given more than his present day's allowance to a beggar at the door. Goodman ' Jackson had been very kind to him, and marvelled much that he had been sent (as) " a servant to the company " and said he " had been better knocked on the head." He entreated his father to redeem him, or at any rate to send provisions which might be sold at a profit, especially cheese, etc. * * * Unless the " Sea-Flower " came in with provisions, his master's men would have but a half-penny loaf for each day's food and might be " turned up to the land and eat bark of trees or moulds of the ground. Therefore, Oh ! that you did see my daily and hourly sighs, groans and tears and thumps that I afford my breast and rue and curse the time of my birth with holy Job. I thought no head had been able to hold so much water as hath and doth daily flow from mine eyes."

The " Sea Flower " was destroyed by an explosion of gunpowder, so that Frethorne's worst misgivings may have been realized.[5]

' Goodman and Goodwife, forms of address then used in England instead of Mr. and Mrs.

[5] Duke of Manchester's MSS. in 8th Report of Royal Commission on Historical MSS.

"THE NEW TOWNE."

HE new policy of the company was carried out by Sir George Yeardley, whose methods were in striking contrast with those of his predecessor, the unprincipled Argall. This marked the beginning of a new era in the colony, of which a feature was " the New Towne," as it was styled in the patents to its residents, with new and better constructed habitations. The term " The New Towne " was applied to about fifty acres on the fourth ridge adjoining on the east the original stockade town of four acres.

One of the thoroughfares of " the New Towne " is referred to in the patents as " the Back Street." As will appear below, " the New Towne " at first comprised the most important part of the corporation, and, as a matter of fact, seems to have been the first substantially built town. Prior to its establishment, land appears not to have been perfectly vested in the settlers. With the beginning of this era and ever after, the place is referred to in the surviving patent transcripts, with the single exception of one of 1664, in which it is called " James Towne," as " James Citty." It is also invariably so referred to in the reports of the meetings of the General or Grand Assembly. The island and containing county were named from the town, the county still bearing the name of James City.

Although the official name of the place was " James Citty," it was generally referred to in official correspondence as " James Towne."

As it is the general opinion that the greater part of the ancient town site has been washed away, it will be a surprise to many to learn that this view is erroneous. The proof of the error is furnished by the old " James Citty " patent records, which, when properly interpreted, show that but a small proportion of the town site has been destroyed, and that the quarter called " the New Towne " has not been encroached on to any appreciable extent by the river. References in some of the patents to branches of "Pitch and Tarr Swamp," and to other topographical features which are probably almost as clearly defined as they were two or three centuries ago, have made it possible to locate the site of "the New Towne," and the greater part of the west end, or old town quarter. Former students of the records have either abandoned them with the conviction that they were too indefinite or obscure for solution, or misconstruing them, evolved incoherent conclusions which have misled and confused the reader. The transcripts pertaining to "James Citty," which are valued principally as old curios, form a labyrinth, in treading which for a long time, a step in any direction led seemingly to hopeless perplexities, and only after repeated and long continued efforts to interpret them, was the "open sesame" found, and a sufficient number linked together to furnish a chart of the ancient town. The period they cover extends from 1619 to 1699. The pages of the record containing two of the earliest and most interesting grants, viz: to Governor Sir George Yeardley, Knt., and Captain Roger Smith, as stated in the introduction, are missing. This will be generally regretted, as possibly on account of their not having been correctly deciphered, the renditions contained in historical publications are not clear.

The method employed in evolving the chart from the patents, although apparently not complicated, was slow, tedious, and replete with failures. Briefly stated, it consisted of finding and uniting plats of different tracts found to have common boundaries. The topography and objects referred to in the patents were platted simultaneously with the boundaries of the land they described.

The incompleteness of the existing records is made apparent by the references in several transcripts to patents which are not of record. Those missing were no doubt improperly entered "in books labelled Bonds, Commissions, Depositions," &c.,[1]

---

[1] *Hening's Statutes*, Vol. II, p. 509.

which were destroyed in the burning of the office of the General Court during the evacuation of Richmond in 1865. Although the records are incomplete, and the descriptions in some of those available contain inaccuracies which required considerable study to correct, while those in others are too meagre or vague to afford any clue to the land's position, they, in many cases, not only furnish the metes and bounds of the area patented, but also a variety of other information, e. g., the ancient names of different localities of the town and island, the positions and directions of the river-bank and highways, the sites of the second fort, called " the turf fort," " the Back Street," in " the New Towne," " the Country House," burned, probably, about 1660, the several statehouse buildings, dwellings of some of the later residents, and other objects now of great interest. A few of the earlier patents record the vocation and social position of the patentee and even the name of the ship in which he came to Virginia, and the year of arrival.

The majority of the plats based on the patents, and represented on the map by solid lines, probably possess about the same degree of accuracy as the work of the average class of compass surveys of to-day. Between 1623 and 1644 only the general directions of land lines are given in the descriptions. About the latter year the surveyors were apparently less inexact and recorded azimuths to the nearest quarter point, or about 2¾ degrees. In a patent of 1656 the azimuths of several sides are given to ⅛ point.

The direction of the Back Street in the Pott patent of 1624 is recorded as " eastward." The azimuth of the street is more definitely stated in the Phips patent, which included the Pott patent, and was issued thirty-two years later, as E. S. E. ¼ S.

Until about 1667 the azimuths of lines were expressed in the same terms as are employed by mariners in boxing the compass. Beginning with the above year, azimuths are given in degrees. By 1683, more careful work appears to have been the rule, and azimuths are recorded to one-fourth of a degree. It would appear from the foregoing that prior to about 1667 some form of the mariner's compass was used in making land surveys, and that about that year the circumferentor came into use.

The consideration on account of which land was granted was always specified in the patent. During the first twenty years it was usually a reimbursement to the patentee of the cost of his own transportation and that of others to the colony, which he had defrayed. The portions of land are styled *devidends*[2] and *dividents,* and were for fifty acres per capita. The grant was conditioned by the annual payment of a nominal sum of money (one shilling per 50 acres) or quantity of tobacco (two to five pounds), designated a fee rent. The fee was made payable in money or tobacco to the "Cape Merchant," as the treasurer was called, either at the feast of St. Michael, the Archangel, or at that of St. Thomas, the Apostle. In at least two of the "James City" patents the specified fee is a capon, "to his Majestie's use," payable "at the feast of St. Thomas the Apostle."[3] A condition named in some patents between 1636 and 1640 is that the patentee should erect a house within six months.[4]

The "James Citty" patents usually describe the grant as being a part of a dividend of fifty acres, or more, situated outside the liberties of the town.

Several patents issued under Cromwell were subsequently confirmed by being re-issued under Charles II.

The transcripts of the patents are the sole remaining evidence authoritatively fixing the initial spot of the nation's history, as almost all other records, including those of the early conveyances, were burned during the War between the States.

The patents relating to "James Citty" are scattered through nine ponderous volumes of MSS. Book I, on account of its antiquity, is the most interesting of the series. As shown by his indorsement at the end of the book, the transcript was made by Edward Harrison in 1683, or nearly a century before the United States attained its independence. The handwriting is clear and

---

[2] This orthography is given in some of the earlier patents.

[3] Virginia Land Patent Records, Book I, p. 689, and Book IV, p. 475.

[4] Virginia Land Patent Records, Book I, p. 689, and Book IV, p. 475.

uniform and to one familiar with the characters then employed, is readily deciphered.

The abbreviation " y " for *th* in *the* and *that* does not appear in this book, which includes the issues up to and during a part of the year 1643. Its first occurrence is in Book VII, in the patent to Edward Chilton, of 1683. The lower case ancient script letter " p " frequently appears as an abbreviation for *per* or *par* in the patents of the entire " James Citty " period.

The second volume is indorsed " Beverly," probably Peter Beverly, who from 1692 to 1700 was clerk of the House of Burgesses, and in the latter year became its speaker. The book was written in 1694. There are no indorsements in the other books to show when they were written or the names of the scriveners.

The first two books were undoubtedly written at " James Citty," and, after escaping the State house fire of 1698, and that of the Capitol at Williamsburg about 1747, were probably moved to Richmond in 1780, when that city became the capital. They have thus passed through two ordeals of fire and two wars and, after silently witnessing many vicissitudes of fortune, rest in the historic Capitol at Richmond.

There does not appear to be any record of legislative enactment defining the limits of " James Citty " except one of " Bacon's Laws," passed in 1676, by which those then existing were extended to include the entire island.[5] The above act, unfortunately, does not recite the previous limits. Shortly after the Bacon uprising was suppressed and the Berkeley government re-instated, the above law was repealed.

Beverly wrote in 1705, that in 1620, the corporations, as they were then styled, were bounded, and that one of the new record books of transcripts contained a statement of Governor Argall to the effect that he had a knowledge of the boundaries of " James Citty." He, however, adds that " there was not to be found one word of the charter or patent itself of the corpora-

---

[5] *Hening's Statutes*, Vol. II, p. 362.

tion." [6]   The patent to Captain John Harvey in 1624 shows that the lower branch of " Pitch and Tarr Swamp " was the town's eastern boundary.

The patents indicate that the town included nearly all of the island above the " Head of Swamp," between James River and the Back River (see map), and that the first and second ridges formed, as it were, outlying districts. They show clearly that after 1623, the most thickly settled part of the town was the " New Towne," on the south shore of the island, below the church.

About the time of Bacon's Rebellion, according to " Bacon's Proceedings," of unknown authorship, in the Burwell MSS. collection,[7] the town was situated " much about the midle of the Sowth line, close upon the River, extending east and west, about 3 quarters of a mile." This description accords with its location as determined from the patents and shown on the map between the initial letters F and G. The church tower, therefore, stood near the western end of the town.

" The New Towne " was situated on the southern slope of the same ridge as the tower ruin (the fourth) and extended east from the first town of four acres, about three-eighths of a mile, to the lower branch of " Pitch and Tarr Swamp." This area is now mostly covered with orchards, in which considerable portions of the ground are filled with particles of brick and mortar of former buildings, scattered by the plow.

Back Street was east of the church and at distances from the south shore of the island varying from two hundred to six hundred feet. The parts of it located were about sixty feet wide,[8] and had the same general direction, east and west, as the highway referred to in the patents as the " way along the Greate River," or " Maine River," which constituted the front street of the " New Towne." The two thoroughfares were connected

[6] *History of the Present State of Virginia,* p. 37.

[7] Force's *Historical Tracts,* Vol. I.

[8] Obtained by platting independently the tracts on opposite sides of the street.

by cross lanes, referred to as highways. The Back Street lay immediately in front of what is believed to have been the site of the Jaquelin-Ambler mansion. It could not have been a street in the modern signification of the word, with sidewalks and pavements, for paving before the doors of houses, even in "London Towne," was not introduced until 1614. It seems to have merged into the "old Greate Road," which led to the head of the island and passed near the northeast corner of the old churchyard, a few rods from the same corner of the present one, near which there appear to be traces of a road.

Traces of the highway along the river-bank, bordered by its gnarled and riven mulberries, lineal descendants, no doubt, of some cited in several patents as reference trees, are still to be seen. The planting of mulberry trees for feeding silkworms was initiated in 1621, and made compulsory by statute. Silk culture received attention as early as 1614, but the enterprise was never a commercial success. Foreign workmen were imported to teach silk making, and a present of silk was sent Charles II by Sir William Berkeley in 1668.[9]

Among the earlier residents of "the New Towne" were some "people of qualitye" and note, including four governors, Sir George Yeardley, Knight; Sir Francis Wyatt, Knight; Sir John Harvey, Knight;" Mister, Governor and Doctor Pott," "Doctor of Physick" and "Physician General to the Colony;" also Captain Ralph Hamor, secretary of state and chronicler; George Sandys, who, while there and residing at William Pierce's (see map), achieved a part of his work of turning into

---

[9] The present of silk, it is stated, was woven into a coronation robe for King Charles. As soon as the king graciously signified his acceptance of the above *douceur*, Sir William presented a petition asking, as a special allowance, the customs duties on a ship's cargo of tobacco. The king adroitly parried this request by sending a warrant for the allowance requested, but payable when Sir William should send to England from Virginia a 300-ton ship laden with silk, hemp, flax, and potatoes. (Sainsbury's Abstracts, June 12, 1669.) It does not appear that the governor ever sent the above shipload of commodities and received the reward.

English Ovid's *Metamorphoses;* Captain Roger Smith, Captain Richard Stevens, who wounded George Harrison in a duel near "James Citty," and George Menify, merchant and member of the council, who married the relict of John Rolfe, whose second wife was Pocahontas. The grounds of the above persons are shown more or less accurately on the map.

Sir George Yeardley's grounds had an area of seven acres, one rood. They were situated on the second ridge between the branch of the swamp and the Back River. The area of Governor Wyatt's tract is not known. It included the ground, where, at a later day, stood the Jaquelin-Ambler mansion. Dr. Pott first patented three acres and a few years later added nine acres. Captain Roger Smith's lot was four acres.

In 1665, there was a bridge across the branch of swamp near the northwest corner of the former twelve acre tract of Governor Pott,[10] connecting the fourth and second ridges. There is a causeway at the above point which may be the successor of the bridge. This probably was the same bridge referred to in the rendition of the Yeardley patent contained on page 68 of Neill's *Virginia Carolorum.*

Sir William Berkeley resided at Jamestown during his first term of office as governor, his residence being one of the brick houses composing the first state house, which stood near the south shore of the island, about one hundred yards east of the eastern boundary of the Association's grounds. The same building appears to have been used by Governor Bennett, who, as the first governor under the Commonwealth, succeeded Berkeley.

Among the later residents of "the New Towne" were Captain George Marable, John Barber, Robert Castle, John Phips, Thos. Woodhouse, John Fitchett, John Knowles and Rev. William Mays. A list of the last residents after Bacon's Rebellion would include the names of Henry Hartwell, clerk of the court, · John Howard, Richard Holder, Lieutenant-Colonel Chiles, John

---

[10] Va. Land Pat. Records, Book V, p. 63.

Page, and although last, not least, Wm. Sherwood, the epitaph on whose tombstone in the little churchyard tells that he was "Born In the Parish Of White Chappell Near London. A Great Sinner Waiting For A Ioyfull Resurrection." Sherwood, during Bacon's Rebellion, was an adherent of Sir William Berkeley. He was attorney-general, 1678-1680. In 1694 he was the proprietor of upwards of three hundred acres of land at the head of the island, including the outlying extreme western part of the town above the upper branch of "Pitch and Tarr Swamp," and a small part of the "New Towne" adjacent to Back Street.

The elevated position of the part of the fourth ridge north of the Back Street, between the site of the Jaquelin-Ambler messuage and the grounds of the Association for the Preservation of Virginia Antiquities, should have made it much sought after for residential purposes. There are some indications of there being house foundations along the line of the Back Street. The names of their occupants can probably never be ascertained, as there are apparently no documents containing that information.

In the address of ex-President Tyler, delivered at Jamestown in 1857 at the celebration of the 250th anniversary of the first landing of the English, he remarked in referring to the destruction of the town by Bacon in 1676: "The town was partially rebuilt, and many of its houses remained during my early novitiate at William and Mary College" (1802-1807). "They stood in a connected street running east and west from near the present dwelling-house (the Jaquelin-Ambler mansion) to the ruins of the church."

The foundations just mentioned probably belonged to the buildings alluded to by President Tyler. "The connected street running east and west" undoubtedly was the Back Street.

"The New Towne" was always inhabited until "James Citty" ceased to exist, the names of various owners of land in that quarter, belonging to different generations, being shown by the patents. Individuals bearing the surnames of many of the former townspeople are still to be found within one hundred miles of the site of "James Citty."

WEST END OF THE TOWN.

HE positions of land grants east of the church tower ruin being determined and the "New Towne" accurately located, investigation was made for the area west of the above ancient landmark. This resulted in placing approximately several early grants, previously referred to, near the head of the island on its western shore and in establishing quite satisfactorily the situation of the Bauldwin grant of 1656, which locates Block House Hill, also in showing the positions of the grants of John Howard, Robert Beverley, the historian, Richard Lawrence, the compatriot of Nathaniel Bacon, Jr., Edward Chilton, attorney-general, Colonel Nathaniel Bacon the elder, Lieutenant Edward Ross, Colonel Philip Ludwell the first,[1] and Philip Ludwell, Esq. (the second), of 1694. The last named grant fixes the position of the last state house.

The tract described is an undated patent to John Howard of about 1690,[2] which Governor Sir Francis Nicholson failed to sign, but which was signed by Governor Sir Edmund Andros in 1694, is approximately located by the present churchyard inclosure (see map).

From the above patent it is learned that the direction of the "old Greate Road" near and north of the churchyard was N. 27¼° W. The marks of this road are visible at the above locality, as before mentioned. Its objective point was probably the isthmus. The parts of the road shown on the map not fixed by the patents are tentative.

---

[1] Philip I was member of the Virginia Council for many years; was expelled therefrom in 1679, reinstated in 1683 and again expelled in 1687 and disqualified for holding office; governor of Carolina 1689-'92; subsequently resided in London and died in England after 1716. Philip II, born 1666, died 1720. Speaker of House and member of council. Buried at Jamestown.

[2] Virginia Land Patent Records, Book VIII, p. 82.

From the Howard patent it is learned that Colonel Nathaniel Bacon, Senior, the second cousin of the patriot of the same name, owned a lot adjoining the Howard tract on the west. It would also appear from agreeing in bearing, that its northern boundary was part of one of the southern boundaries of part of a lot that once belonged to the scholarly Lawrence, sequestered on account of its owner's participation in Bacon's Rebellion, and bought by Colonel Bacon, Senior, in 1683—possibly because it adjoined his tract, which was in front of the present tower ruin. Lawrence's house, according to T. M.'s account of Bacon's Rebellion,[3] was one of the finest in the town. The remainder of the Lawrence tract probably extended east of that bought by Bacon. On using the common boundary line of the Howard and Lawrence plats, and placing the former in what appears to be its proper position near the graveyard, the latter is found to have for its northern boundary the branch of "Pitch and Tarr Swamp," which accords with the description in the patent.

The patent of the Lawrence tract[4] fixes the position, as its western boundary, of a grant to Robert Beverley in 1694, which in turn furnishes the position of "The Maine Cart road," probably another name for "the old Greate Road," leading, most probably, past the well about one rod east of the state house foundations on the third ridge, towards the isthmus and Block House Hill.

A correspondence of the course of the western line of a tract granted to William Edwards[5] in 1690 with that of the eastern line of the Chilton tract locates the Edwards tract, and through it the western line of a lot of Nathaniel Bacon, Senior. The eastern boundary of the Bacon tract, as has been pointed out, was the Howard tract. Bacon's lot, therefore, occupied the greater part of the eastern half of the space on which stands the Confederate fort of 1861.

---

[3] Force's *Historical Tracts*, Vol. I.
[4] Virginia Land Patent Records, Book VII, p. 300.
[5] *Ibid*, Book VIII, p. 42.

The locating of the third and fourth state houses was accom-plished by determining the approximate positions of two land grants on a modern map of the head of the island, followed by probing and excavating.

Extracts from the patents are as follows:

Phillip Ludwell, April 20, 1694,—1½ acres. Va. Land Patent Records, Book VIII, p. 315.

"One Acre and halfe of Land adjoyning to the Ruins of his three Brick houses between the State house and Country house in James City which Land is bounded Viz. beginning Neare Pitch and Tarr Swamp Eight Cheynes of the East'most end of the said houses and running by the said end south two degrees westerly Sixteen cheynes thence North Eighty Eight degrees Westerly three and three quarter Cheynes thence North two degrees Easterly sixteen Cheynes by the other End of the said houses and thence South Eighty Eight degrees Easterly three and three quarter cheynes to the place it begun."

Edward Chilton, April 16, 1683,—2 acres, 17 chains. Va. Land Patent Records, Book VII, p. 292.

" bounded, viz: from Col. Phillip Ludwells corner stake south eighty-eight degrees, easterly partly along his Hon^{rs} line ninety fouer chaines, thence south fouer degrees, and an halfe westerly, partly along an old ditch twelve chaines and an halfe down James river bank and along under ye said Hill to a stake neer ye brick fort, and thence north sixteen degrees easterly seaven cha: and an halfe to ye first stake."

The tract of Philip Ludwell being platted, its most probable location, after correcting for declination the bearings of its lines as given in the patent, was found to be on the third ridge, near the then southern end of the seawall. This was decided upon after considerable study and reflection, taking into account the distance from " Pitch and Tarr Swamp " of the crest of the third ridge, which appeared to be a good site for the three houses shown by the patent to have been on the tract. Although the above location seemed to be the only one which would meet the requirements of the patent, it was not finally accepted until, as shown later, it was confirmed by further investigation.

The tract of Edward Chilton was next platted. A clue to its location was furnished by one of its boundary lines terminating "neer ye brick fort," which fort, in 1688, was described by the Rev. John Clayton as being situated in "a vale," above the town, and consequently, above the church tower. A probable position for the brick fort, fulfilling the conditions imposed by the above description, seemed to be in the extension westward from the river bank of the swale between the third and fourth ridges. This view was confirmed by the discovery, by sounding, of piles of masonry in the shallow water at the locality named. The Chilton tract thus being approximately located with reference to the brick fort, valuable information was furnished as to the character and direction of the shore line, a "Hill" [high bank] lying about east and west. A most important and interesting feature, however, is yet to be noted, viz., that when the Chilton tract was given its most probable location on the map, it was found to connect with the assumed location of Philip Ludwell's tract. Moreover, the northern boundary of the Chilton tract which passed "partly along his Hon'rs line" (Hon. Philip Ludwell) is shown by the patents to have the same magnetic bearing as the southern boundary of the Philip Ludwell tract of 1694. The grantee of the 1694 tract, entitled Philip Ludwell, Esq., was undoubtedly the son of the Hon. Philip Ludwell referred to in the Chilton patent. It seems probable that Philip Ludwell the second received part of his grant of 1694, the southern, from his father, who owned it in 1683, and possibly also the three brick houses, for the patent implies that the houses belonged to the second Ludwell before its date of issue in 1694.

The patent of 1694 states that Philip Ludwell, Esq., had land due him for the transportation of one person to Virginia, and he naturally selected a new piece adjacent to that which he then held, probably north of the houses, receiving a grant for the new and old tracts combined. Instances are found in the old patent records of a patent being issued covering earlier grants that were contiguous to that acquired at the time of issuing the later patent.

The proximity of the first Philip Ludwell's property to the state house may account, to some extent, for the interest which he had in rebuilding the state house destroyed by Bacon, for which work he was, in fact, the contractor.

The plats of Chilton and Ludwell being thus united, trial was made to ascertain if the combined plats could be better located when platted separately. It was found, however, that no change could be made that would improve the first location, and the author concluded that the time had arrived to verify his work by examining the ground. An opportunity for doing this occurred in January, 1903, when, to his great satisfaction, and that of a co-worker, the steel probe used for exploring the ground, struck a number of buried foundation walls. The subsequent work of the Association for the Preservation of Virginia Antiquities, under his direction, has confirmed his views, the foundations discovered being within less than twenty-five feet of their position as indicated by the Ludwell patent, and having the same width collectively as given for the Ludwell tract. Moreover, after correcting for variation of the needle, the different walls were found to have about the same azimuths as the boundaries of the Ludwell tract, given in the patent.

Adjoining the Ludwell house foundations on the east are others agreeing in a general way with the meagre descriptions extant of the state house, and to the west others, which are, of course, the remains of the " Country House " of 1694.

Further references to the above state house and brick fort are made under their respective captions.

Near the lower extremity of the seawall, and just outside of it, formerly stood a brick building, which Richard Randolph stated in 1837 was reputed to have been a powder magazine.[6] This building was referred to in ex-President Tyler's address at

---

[6] *Southern Literary Messenger*, Vol. III, p. 303.

Jamestown in 1857,[7] previously quoted from, as the prison house of Opechancanough, brother of the great Powhatan. He also stated that its cellar had been formerly used for the storage of powder. If used as a magazine, uncommonly bad judgment was displayed in placing it where it would have been such a good target for a hostile fleet and where also in event of an explosion, it would have damaged or destroyed the buildings on the third ridge. The allusion to it as the prison of Opechancanough is suggestive of its being used as a jail, although probably not for the Indian chief who died a captive at Jamestown about two years after the massacre of 1644.

In 1891 the eastern foundation wall was all that remained of the reputed "magazine." It was then located and found to be about thirty-two feet long. If it was a prison, it probably was not built until after 1685, in which year the subject of building a prison was brought up in the Assembly; if a magazine, it was probably erected at an earlier date, possibly about the time that the brick fort, hereinafter described, was constructed.

Incidentally, it may be stated that the third ridge was used as a camp ground for Confederate soldiers in 1861.

[7] Celebration of the 250th anniversary of the English settlement at Jamestown, May 13, 1857.

Church Buildings and Original Graveyard of the "Mother Christian Towne."

ONE of the vexed questions concerning the first settlement is the position of the first churchyard or graveyard. It is learned from several old chronicles that the first church was within the triangular fort. The map of the Virginia settlement, procured by Zuñiga, for Philip III of Spain, in September, 1608, previously referred to, shows a church thus inclosed.

The first church, a rude hut "covered with rafts, sedge and earth," was burned within eight months of its erection. The second, erected in 1608, most probably on the same site as the first, must also have been a flimsy makeshift, for it is referred to by Sir Thomas Gates, two years after its construction, as being in an unserviceable condition, shortly after which it was reconstructed by Lord La Warr. Its dimensions in plan were sixty feet long by twenty-four feet wide, with a steeple at the west end.

As the greater part of the triangular fort, as has been pointed out, has been washed away, the site of the second church is now probably under water. No vestige of its foundations have been, or probably ever will be discovered.

When, in 1617, Captain Argall arrived at "James Towne," he discovered the church which La Warr had renovated seven years before in ruins, a storehouse being in use for divine service. During his administration, *i. e.,* from May, 1617, to April, 1619, the third church, whose dimensions were "50 by 20 foote," was erected.

In 1639 Governor Sir John Harvey wrote to the Privy Council: "Such hath bene our Indeavour herein, that out of our owne purses wee have largely contributed to the building of a brick church, and both Masters of Shipps and others of the

5—J. T.

ablest Planters have liberally by our persuation underwritt to this worke." [1]

No information is available as to when the building of this, the fourth church, was begun or completed, but the latter is supposed to have been accomplished by about 1647. It was burned in 1676.

There is apparently no evidence as to whether this building was entirely or partly destroyed by the fire. It is probable that only the wood work, i. e., the roof and window and door frames, were burned. There is no information when the building was rehabilitated. It is presumed, however, to have been done during the partial rebuilding of the town between 1676 and 1686. The building was apparently used until about the end of the 18th century, about which time its walls fell, and the bricks composing them were used by Mr. William Lee, of Green Spring, and Mr. John Ambler, of Jamestown, to inclose a part of the old burial ground. The greater part of the graveyard walls are still standing.

In his *Old Churches and Families of Virginia,* Bishop Meade states, with reference to the foundations of the last brick church, which he measured during a visit to Jamestown Island shortly before 1856, that the plan of the church was that of a basilica, whose accurately measured dimensions were twenty-eight by fifty-six feet. [2]

In the summer of 1901, the above foundations which adjoin the eastern wall of the tower ruins, were uncovered by Mr. John Tyler, Jr., under the auspices of the Association for the Preservation of Virginia Antiquities, to which society the surrounding tract of twenty-three acres belongs. [3] The average length and width within the walls are fifty and six-tenths feet and twenty-two and seven-tenths feet, respectively.

---

[1] Letter from Governor and Council in Virginia to Privy Council. *McDonald Papers,* Vol. II, pp. 233-260.

[2] Meade's *Old Churches and Families of Virginia,* Vol. I, p. III.

[3] Donated to the above association by Mr. and Mrs. Edward E. Barney, in 1895.

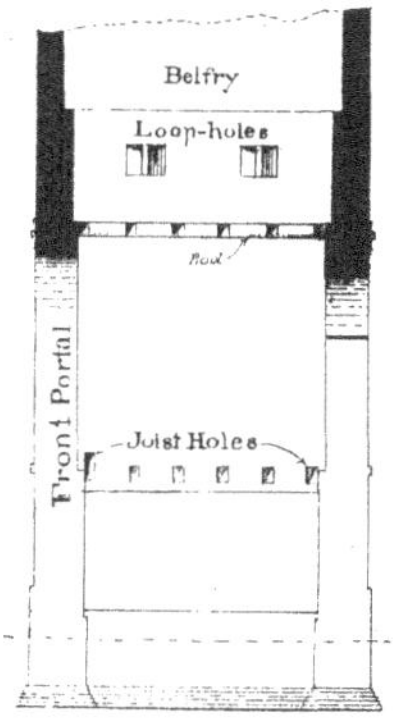

Fig.3

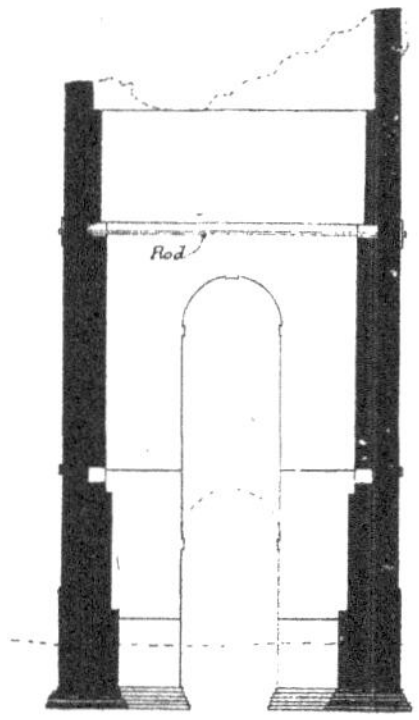

Belfry

Loop-holes

Rod

Joist Holes

Front Portial

Fig.4

Rod

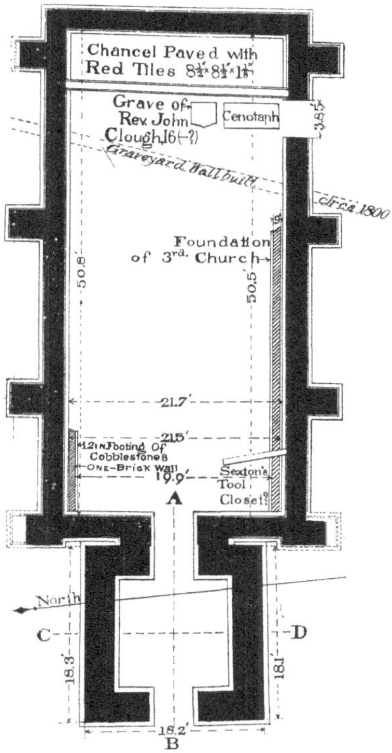

Chancel Paved with
Red Tiles 8½×8½×1½

Grave of
Rev. John
Clough 16(-?)

Cenotaph

3.85

Graveyard Wall built

Circa 1800

Foundation
of 3rd. Church

50.8'

50.5'

15'

21.7'

21.5'

12.i.n.footing of
Cobblestones
One-Brick Wall

19.2'

A

Sexton's
Tool
Closet?

North

C

D

18.3'

18.1'

18.2'

B

Fig.1

Explanation:

Fig. 1 = Foundation Plan of
Fourth Church Structure
Inclosing Fragments of
Foundations of Third.
Broken Lines Show Cor-
rect Positions of But-
tresses.
Fig. 2 Front of Tower.
Fig. 3 Section on Line A-B.
Fig. 4   ,,   ,,   ,, C-D.

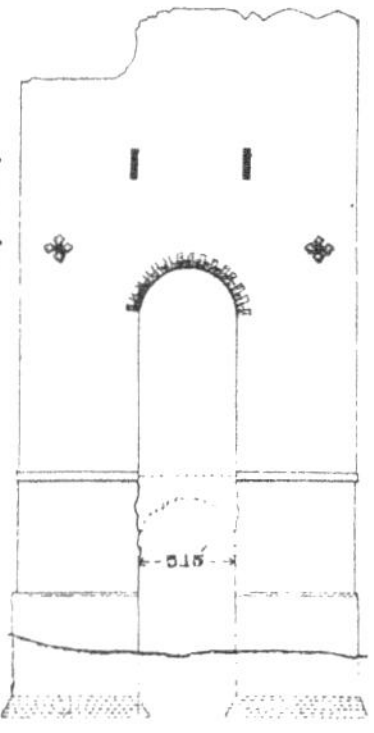

5.10'

Fig.2

RUINS OF
CHURCH STRUCTURES
ERECTED AT
IAMES CITTY, VA.
ABOUT 1617 AND 1639.

SCALE.

0 2 4 6 8 10 12 Ft.
  1 3 5 7 9 11

In clearing away from around the foundations the mould of more than a century, parts of the foundations of the side walls of a narrower building, whose inside width was about twenty feet, were uncovered. They consist of a footing of cobble-stones one foot thick, capped by a one-brick wall. The slenderness of the foundations indicates that their superstructure was of timber, as in the days of substantial building to which they belonged, they would have been regarded as too light for one of brick. It will be observed that the width of a building matching the foundations would be the same as given for the church built during Argall's term as deputy-governor. As only the western ends of the foundations of the two side walls remain, the length of the building they supported cannot be learned.

In making the before-mentioned excavations it is reported that three distinct sets of floor tiles were found at different levels across the east end of the building, formerly belonging to a chancel five and one-half feet by twenty-two feet, indicating that there were three church structures on the same site. The lowest layer of tiles probably belonged to the third church and, in that case, if its end walls were inclosed in the same manner as its side walls, which seems quite likely, the length of the third church would have been about fifty feet.

As the same site was used for the three church buildings erected after 1617, the churchyard, which was by custom the principal burial ground, most probably was never changed, and was probably used even before that year. The finding of a human skeleton, while excavating the foundations, crossed by a wall of the brick church near its southeastern corner, shows that there was a burial ground at its site before the first brick church was built (1639-1647), and possibly even before the building of the timber church about 1618, which covered almost all of the ground occupied by its successor.

From what has preceded there should be no room for doubt as to the lighter foundations being those of the third church structure, that built under Argall, and in use when Yeardley came to the colony in 1619. The inclosure of one structure by

the other suggests that, while the later church of brick was
being constructed around the earlier one of timber, the latter
was used for service.

As the marriage of John Rolfe to Pocahontas occurred in
1614, it would appear that the ceremony could not have been
performed in the third church, whose site, as shown above, was
subsequently occupied by the brick churches, but in the second
structure, 60 by 24 feet in plan, which was reconstructed by
Lord La Warr, and situated within the triangular fort a short
distance, probably one hundred and thirty yards, above the
church tower. The third church, however, was undoubtedly
the one used for the convening of the first American legislature
by Governor Yeardley, on July 30, 1619.[4]

Although the first and second churches were within the triangular fort, it is not probable that the graveyard was. To have
lived continually in such close proximity to their probable ulti-
mate resting place would have been as distasteful to the settlers
as to most people of this day. Moreover, the available area of
the acre inclosure, as already demonstrated, would have been
fully occupied by the buildings and streets mentioned by Strachey. Interments would have been made near, but outside of
the triangular fort. By the time the third church was erected,
about 1618, the burial ground, in consequence of the frightful
mortality, must have grown to considerable proportions, and no
site could have seemed more appropriate for it than the ground
contiguous to that which had been consecrated as " God's
Acre."

On the occasion of the celebration at Jamestown of the
bicentenary of the advent of the English,[5] " as it were by
general consent the discovery of the oldest stone became an
object of general emulation." * * * "beyond 1682, nothing
legible could be traced, but from the freshness of the marble

---

[4] *Colonial Records of Virginia*, Extra Senate (State) Document of
1874.

[5] *Report on the Proceedings of the Late Jubilee at Jamestown, Va.*,
page 9.

IN THE CHURCHYARD

The sycamore tree in the middle ground grew between the tombs of Rev. James Blair, Commissary to the Bishop of London, and his wife and shattered the stones. The injury being done to the tombs was observed at the Bi-Centenary celebration in 1807.

bearing this date contrasted with the surrounding masses of mutilated and mouldering decay, it was the general impression that this stone was comparatively young." As, ordinarily, gravestones do not become illegible in less than one hundred and fifty to two hundred years, the assumption is not unreasonable that some of those seen at Jamestown in 1807 belonged to the same period as the third church, although the earliest known date on any tombstone in Virginia is 1637.[6] There is very good evidence that until about the 18th century many of the tombstones used in Virginia were shipped from across seas.

It is stated by some who were present at Sunday services held for the island garrison in the old churchyard in 1861 that there was then a sufficient number of tombstones to serve as seats for the command of two hundred men. Only a few complete stones remain, and the fragments of others show what has been the common fate of nearly all.

Reference is now made to two grants to " Thomas Hampton, Clerke," in 1639 and 1644.[7] Both tracts are described as being on a ridge of land behind the church, the earlier and smaller between two swamps and the later " containing from the Eastermost bounds Westerly one hundred and twelve paces five foot to the pace and running the same Breadth Northerly to the back river." The later grant may have been made to include the earlier, a practice which, as previously noted, was common to the period. In any event, both grants were most probably upon the same ridge.

Several patents are employed to locate Hampton's two tracts, as follows: to John Bauldwin in 1656 for 15 acres 69 poles, 5 acres 69 poles of which were " at the old block house " and ten acres bounded " Easterly upon Mr. James' land Northerly upon the back river " [marsh?], and the smaller tract, " West upon the Main river and South upon the slash which lyeth between the State house and the said Mr. James." James' western

---

[6] Colonel Wm. Perry's at Westover. Colonel Perry was member of House of Burgesses and subsequently member of the Council.

[7] Virginia Land Patent Records, Book I, p. 689, and Book II, p. 105.

boundary was a meridian passing " by Friggett landing." [8]   The approximate position of "Friggett Landing" is learned from the probable position of a grant to Richard Clarke in .1646.[9]

In 1644 Richard Sanders patented an acre "bounded west upon the river East upon ye marsh North upon the block house land and South upon the Land of Edward Challos." In the same year Edward Challis received a grant of an acre bounded "West upon the river East upon the marsh North upon the blockhouse Land and South towards the land of Radulph Spraggon." The word "upon" in the phrase "upon the blockhouse land" in the Challos patent should be *towards,* for Challos is given as the southern boundary of Sanders in the latter's patent. Spraggon's land, an acre, patented in 1644, was bounded "South upon the land of Geo. Gilbert North towards the Way leading towards the Mayne West upon the river and East towards the land of Mr. Hampton." Bauldwin's patent shows approximately the former site of Block House Hill, below which was the land of Sanders, adjoining whom on the south was Challos. Next below came a space, probably unoccupied except by part of the highway, below which, but not adjoining, was Spraggon, all about as shown on the "Map of Iames Citty."

Arguments have been presented for the sites of the churches used after 1617 and of the graveyard pertaining to them before that year, as being adjacent to the tower ruin at the eastern side of the four-acre paled town.

The description of an acre granted to John White in 1644 reads, " bounded West upon the Church Yard East upon the land apprtaining to the State House North towards the land of Mr. Thomas Hampton and South upon James River the Length being twenty three poles and breadth Seaven poles almost."

The word "towards" in the White patent and also in the Spraggon patent with reference to Hampton's land, shows that the last named was situated north of the first and east of the

---

[8] Virginia Land Patent Records, Book IV, p. 196.

[9] *Ibid,* Book II, p. 47.

second, but in each case at some indefinite, but not remote distance, the intervening land not being patented. By projecting
series of lines east from Spraggon and north from White they
will intersect on the second ridge about where the Hampton
land is indicated on the map.

On account of the peculiar wording of the parts of the Hampton patents, describing the relative positions of the tracts on a
ridge, and the church, viz.; " behind the church," it is not clear
at first glance whether the church and the tracts were on the
same, or different ridges. If on the same, the second, the
church would have been mentioned in Spraggon's patent, whose
land was west of Hampton's. No allusion to the church, however, occurs in that or any other patent on or near the western
shore of the island. The particle " behind " is not understood
as meaning in the rear of the church's back wall, but signifying
on the opposite side from where the writer stood or imagined
he was standing, or possibly as having reference to some other
object understood but not mentioned, e. g., the churchyard or
river bank. The above is a sample of the vague and inaccurate
expressions appearing in some of the patents and too often used
at the present day.

As, according to its description, the White tract was on the
southern bank of the island and the churchyard adjoined it on
the west, the latter was also on the river bank. Finally, until
1644 the first ridge belonged to the block house, and the land
at the western end of the second ridge has been accounted for
in that year; the third ridge was occupied by buildings from an
early day (1666), and, therefore, most probably never contained
the church or graveyard; all of which also goes to show that the
church and graveyard were not on the western bank of the
island. All of the available evidence pertaining to the church,
therefore, proves that it and the graveyard, in 1644, were on the
fourth ridge and on the southern water front at the old tower
ruin.

Bishop Meade states in effect that the graves near the tower
ruin inclosed by a brick wall, before referred to, near the close

of the eighteenth century, cover but a third of the original graveyard, which had an area of a half acre. Although the graves are in very close order, each one apparently occupying, on an average, about thirty-two square feet, it is evident that a half-acre would have sufficed but for a small fraction of those who died at " James Citty." [10]

In 1896, as before described, the remnant of the original headland, which still shielded the adjacent river bank below it from abrasion, was removed to bring the shore to a fair line for receiving protection work, constructed in that year. It is credibly stated that when the bank thus exposed was undermined by the waves, several human skeletons lying in regular order, east and west, about two hundred feet west of the tower ruin were uncovered. On account of their nearness to the tower it seems quite probable that the skeletons were in the original churchyard. One of the skulls had been perforated by a musket ball and several buckshot, which it still held, suggesting a military execution. Soon after being exposed to the air the skeletons crumbled.

From the evidence of the White patent and the positions of the skeletons, it would appear that the churchyard extended from the junction of the Back Street with the " old Greate Road," northeast of the church, to near the water side and up the latter, including a part of the ground subsequently covered by the Confederate fort. Thus situated, it would have had an area of about one and one-half acres.

Judging from the brick bond of the church tower it belonged originally to the fourth of the five churches, all of which, except the latest one, are more or less briefly referred to in the available annals of the colonists.

The brick church would to-day be regarded as a very plain and unpretentious chapel. It was rectangular in plan, having the customary high pitched roof on both nave and tower, the aisle paved with brick and the chancel with tiles. The tower,

---

[10] Meade's *Old Churches and Families of Virginia*, Vol. I, p. III.

THE TOWER RUIN

situated at the western end, on account of being dispro-portionately large in comparison with the rest of the struc-ture, was the prominent feature. On account of its solidity, it was not materially injured by the conflagration of 1676. Arched doorways through the front and back walls of the first story formed the main entrance. The second story openings were most probably a window in the west wall and a door in the east wall, the latter opening into a gallery across the western end of the nave, as in the " old Brick Church " at Smithfield, Va. The third story was probably lighted only by six loop holes, two in the front and two in each side wall. The loop holes indicate that the intention of the builders of the tower was to make it defensible against Indian attack. As, with the defeat and death of Opechancanough in 1644, the fear of such attacks occurring at Jamestown should have almost entirely dis-appeared, it seems likely that the tower was designed and prob-ably built before or about that time. The brick work formerly separating the openings of the first and second stories having broken away, the front and back walls now have high portals extending to about twenty and nineteen feet, respectively, above the ground.

The brick work of the tower and foundation is in so-called English bond, quaintly embelished, after the fashion of the period, with glazed headers. The walls of the ruin were recently strengthened by tie rods, with ornamental washers of cruciform shape. It is a dignified old pile, of sombre detail, and originally had a height of about forty-six feet, to the peak of the spire that surmounted it. It is approximately eighteen feet square in plan, with walls three feet thick at the base, diminishing by offsets in the inner faces at each story to about seventeen inches at the belfry.

Within nave and chancel are interred many unknown dead, and, lying with its head to the north, is an ironstone tablet from which are missing inlaid brasses with which it was embossed. In its present position it does not apear to mark a tomb, for it would thus show a violation of the time-revered custom, formerly universally observed in Christian burials, to place the feet towards the rising sun. Whose "death in life" it commemorated will probably ever remain one of the unsolved mysteries of this mysterious island. This tomb stone is probably the only one in this country that had brasses. In the upper sinister corner was the escutcheon of the deceased. The scroll in the upper dexter corner was probably inscribed with a text or short prayer. It is conjectured by some that the stone formerly marked the grave of Governor, Sir George Yeardley, Knight, who died at Jamestown Nov. 12, 1627. The Rev. John Clough whose grave stone is shown on the plan of the church, was condemned to death by Nathaniel Bacon, "the Rebel," but was not executed.

The "James Citty" brick church resembled the "old Brick Church" about five miles from Smithfield, Isle of Wight County, Virginia, modernly known as St. Luke's. The latter, however, is a larger building than was the former. The points in common between the two churches are a tower at the western end, and a chancel door on the south side, near the eastern end of the nave. The brick work of St. Luke's church, however, is laid in so-called Flemish bond, and its tower has quoins at the corners, broad friezes at each story and under the eaves and its exterior faces broken by offsets at each story.

THE MYSTERIOUS TABLET.

The tablet is 5 feet 7¾ inches long by 31¼ inches wide. The black surfaces show the channelings in the stone formerly filled with metal. The inscription plate was about 19 by 10¼ inches, and the height of the draped figure 24⅝ inches.

THE COLONIAL LEGISLATURE.

WHEN Captain Smith became president of the colony, in 1608, he styled the meeting of the colonists which he called to announce that thereafter those who would not work must starve, a "generall assembly." [1]

A peculiar feature of the first colonial legislature, and apparently of those of many ensuing years, was that both of its branches, the governor's council and the House of Burgesses, met in joint session, after the fashion of the Scotch Parliament.

According to Beverley, this custom obtained until 1680, when Governor Culpeper, "taking advantage of some disputes among them," caused the two bodies to hold their sessions in separate apartments,[2] the council being presided over by the governor and the House of Burgesses by a speaker of its own election.

It was resolved at a session of the House of Burgesses in March, 1658, that "they"—"all propositions and lawes"—"shall be first discussed among the Burgesses only" * * * "in private" * * * "and not in presence of the Governour and Council."[3] The above action of the burgesses, evincing a desire to assert the independence of their body, was a precursor of the discontinuance of joint sessions, above noted by Beverley.

From what follows, the custom of holding joint sessions apparently had been discontinued before 1680, although it had been customary for two of the members of the council to attend the sessions of the burgesses, as shown in " T. M.'s "[4] account of Bacon's Rebellion.

---

[1] *Works, Captain John Smith*, p. 149.

[2] *History of the present State of Virginia*, by Robert Beverley, p. 187.

[3] *Hening's Statutes*, Vol. I, p. 497.

[4] *The Beginning, Progress and Conclusion of Bacon's Rebellion in Virginia, in the Years* 1675-1676, p. 13.—*Force's Historical Tracts*, Vol. I.—" T. M." is supposed by Campbell and Fiske to have been

The ostensible purpose of the presence of the councillors was to assist the burgesses in conducting their proceedings in a parliamentary manner. The real object, obviously, was to keep the governor fully apprised of all that occurred in this democratic and often intractable body. This was fully understood by the burgesses, some of whom on the occasion referred to by " T. M.," manifested their unwillingness to have the councillors present.

Prior to its session in September, 1632, the colonial legislature of Virginia was styled " The General Assembly." Beginning with the above session, it was called " The Grand Assembly," which title it bore until the session of June, 1680, when the former appellation was revived.

Thomas Mathews, son of Samuel Mathews, governor of Virginia, 1657-1659. (Campbell's *History of Virginia*, p. 284, and Fiske's *Old Virginia and her Neighbors*, Vol. II, p. 66.) The available evidence is quite conclusive that " T. M." was Thomas Mathew, and not Thomas Mathews, a son of the governor. See Notes and Queries, by W. G. Stanard, *Virginia Historical Magazine*, Vol. I. (1893-1894), pp. 201 and 202. He was a timid, cautious man, who unwillingly became the representative of Stafford county in the first Assembly after the " Long Assembly."

"James Citty" State Houses.

THE first General Assembly, as previously stated, was convened in the third church, referred to in a preceding chapter as having its foundations inclosed by those of its successor, the first brick church, erected between 1639 and 1647.

The available information concerning the various buildings used for subsequent meetings of the legislature and for holding courts is too incomplete, meagre and obscure to be reduced to a succinct and entirely satisfactory statement. Following are deductions from the available data pertinent to the subject, which are given in subsequent pages:

During about the first two decades after 1619 there were at least twelve sessions of the legislature. They were probably held either in the third church or at the governor's house. There were also held during the above period sessions of the court and meetings of the governor and council. From the latter the proclamations of the governor that were intended to take the place of legislative enactments, were probably promulgated.[1]

During the next six decades, while "James Citty" remained the seat of government, there were apparently four different state house buildings, all of which were burned. The time they were occupied collectively amounted to about forty-three years. During the intervals between the burning of the several statehouses and the acquiring of new ones, amounting in the aggregate approximately to seventeen years, taverns were used for the meetings of the Assembly and the sessions of the courts.

As in April, 1641, the colonial government purchased from ex-Governor Harvey, who about a year before was adjudged a bankrupt, one of his houses, known as the courthouse, the

---

[1] *Hening's Statutes*, Vol. I, p. 120.

courts and meetings of the governor and council were no doubt held there, and probably also the meetings of the whole legislature. The above building, therefore, most probably constituted the first state house.

In June, 1642, the Grand Assembly presented Governor Berkeley with two houses and a tract of land adjacent to them, at "James Citty." Between the above year and 1655, Governor Berkeley erected a house adjoining on the west the first state house, which thus became the middlemost of three houses, all having the same dimensions in plan, viz., forty by twenty feet, and forming a block with a frontage on the river of sixty feet and a depth of forty feet. The block was sixty-seven feet from the southern bank of the island and about forty-five yards below the present wharf. The bank probably having receded slightly, its site would now be somewhat nearer the present bank line.

The middle house of the block was used as a state house for about thirteen years longer, or until some time between March, 1655, and June, 1656, when it would seem to have been burned. After the burning of the above building two courts were held in a tavern kept by Thomas Woodhouse.

The available information about the second state house is scant and indirect. The building appears to have been acquired some time before October, 1656. All that is known of it is learned from a reference to it in a patent of the above year from which it appears to have been situated on the fourth ridge. It apparently was used for but three or four years, and then burned.

During the ensuing five years, or until about 1665, the colony's affairs seem to have been transacted in part, if not entirely, in taverns belonging to Thomas Woodhouse and Thomas Hunt, situated on the river bank about one hundred and three hundred yards respectively, east of the first state house. About the above year a house was purchased or built by the colonial government on the third ridge about two hundred and forty yards northwest of the brick church, and this served as the state house until burned by Nathaniel Bacon, Jr., in September, 1676.

During the ten years following, or until about 1686, the expedient of using taverns for meetings of the legislature was again resorted to. In the above year the re-building of the state house was completed. As it was on the site of its predecessor, it most probably had the same proportions, which in plan were about seventy-four feet long and twenty feet wide, within the walls. This was the last state house building erected at "James Citty." It was occupied for about twelve years, and was burned in the fall of 1698. The Assembly held its last session at "James Citty," in April, 1699, when it was decreed to move the capital to Williamsburg.

Subjoined are the data on which the foregoing is based.

The earliest available evidence of the colony's intention to build a state house appears in a letter from its governor, Sir John Harvey, Knight, and his council to the Privy Council, dated January 18, 1639, in which it is stated that by the king's command a levy had been raised for the above purpose.[2] One year later, during the session of the Grand Assembly beginning January 6, 1639-40,[3] an act was passed providing for defraying the cost of building a state house by a poll assessment of two pounds of tobacco.

On April 7, 1641, about fifteen months after the passage of the above act, Sir John Harvey conveyed to the colonial government, for 15,700 pounds of tobacco, to be paid the following January,[4] " all that capital messuage or tenement now used for a court house late in the tenure of Sir John Harvey, Knt.,

---

[2] *McDonald Papers*, Vol. I, p. 249.

[3] *Hening's Statutes*, Vol. I, p. 226.—The acts of several of the Assemblies between 1619 and 1642 are not known to be in existence. They are only known to have been framed by allusions to them in acts passed at other sessions, contained in *Hening's Statutes*, and from being mentioned in the land patents, in official correspondence, and in the minutes of the London Company.

[4] The poll assessment of January, 1640, would have become due January, 1641.

situate and being within James City Island in Virginia with the old house and granary, garden and orchard as also one piece or plot of ground lying and being on the west side of the said capital and messuage as the same is now inclosed." [5] The above conveyance shows that the court had been holding its sessions in a house owned by Sir John Harvey, and it seems quite likely that the assessment of January, 1639-40, was expended in buying Harvey's houses and lot, one of the former being the court house. It is more than possible that the Grand Assembly had also been meeting in the same house. It seems most probable that the above building was the one mentioned in patents referred to below as "the old state house," whose location is given further on.

In a letter of instructions from King Charles I to Governor Berkeley and the Colonial Council in August, 1641, the building of a state house is ordered.

By an act of Assembly passed in June, 1642, two houses and an orchard "belonging to the colony" were presented to Governor Berkeley. This act was confirmed by another passed at the session of March, 1642. [6]

In February, 1643, a patent was issued to Captain Robert Hutchinson, burgess from "James Citty," for one and one-half acres situated on the south shore of the island and bounded west in part "towards" the state house. [7] It appears from the Hutchinson patent that by 1643 the previous acts of Assembly for procuring a state house had gone into effect, and that the building was on the south shore of the island.

---

[5] Transcripts of Miscellaneous MSS., by Conway Robinson, p. 188.

[6] *Hening's Statutes*, Vol. I, p. 267.

[7] Va. Land Pat. Records, Book I, p. 944.

Hutchinson's patent reads " bounded South upon the river North towards Pasby Hayes, West upon the land of John Osborne & 'towards the State House." As the tract could not have been situated on the southern bank of the island and at the same time been in a southerly direction from Paspahegh town, which was on the main land above the island, either some other locality named Pasby Hayes was referred to or an error made in describing the tract or transcribing the patent.

In August, 1644, a patent previously quoted from was issued to John White for one acre of land lying along the south shore of the island, between the churchyard on the west and the state house land on the east.[8] This locates the state house with reference to the churchyard in 1644, whose position has already been determined, and places the western boundary of the state house grounds about twelve yards below the present wharf, or about seventy yards below the eastern boundary of the land now owned by the Association for the Preservation of Virginia Antiquities.

On March 30, 1655, Sir William Berkeley sold to Richard Bennett, who had succeeded him as governor in 1652, his house, " the westernmost of the three brick houses," which the deed recites the grantor had built.[9] The deed, however, does not show that the ground on which the house stood and that adjacent to it was sold with the house. The above mentioned land was granted to Thomas Ludwell and Thomas Stegge, January 1, 1667. Its area was a half acre. It was situated on the southern shore of the island " adjoining to the westermost of those three houses all of which joyntly were formerly called by the name of the old state house," sixty-seven feet from high-water mark.[10] From what follows the patent apparently did not include the house, or, more correctly, its ruins.

Henry Randolph, clerk of the court, sold the ruins of the three houses and the grounds they respectively covered, April 7, 1671,[11] as follows: The eastern house ruins and grounds to Thomas Swann, of the county of Surry; the middle, or " old state house " proper, to Nathaniel Bacon [Sr.], executor of the estate of Colonel Myles Cary,[12] and the western to Thomas

---

[8] Va. Land Pat. Records, Book II, p. 10.

[9] *Hening's Statutes*, Vol. I, p. 407.

[10] *Virginia Land Patent Records*, Book VI, p. 223.

[11] *Conway Robinson's Transcripts of Miscellaneous Manuscripts*, p. 258, from *General Court Rule Book No. 2*, pp. 155, 617.

[12] Colonel Cary came to Virginia in 1645, constructed the first fort on site of Fort Monroe, and was killed there in an engagement with the Dutch, in 1667.

Ludwell. By his will, proved May 15, 1671, Thomas Stegge left to Thomas Ludwell his interest in a house bought jointly with Ludwell of Henry Randolph.[13] Ludwell subsequently secured a patent for a half acre of land adjoining the house ruins and sold the property to Sir William Berkeley for one hundred and fifty pounds sterling, March 17, 1672.[14]

It seems most probable that the building erected by Governor Berkeley between 1642 and 1655 and sold by him to Richard Bennett in the latter year, the one referred to in the patent to Ludwell and Stegge of 1667, that sold by Randolph to Thomas Ludwell in 1671, and by Ludwell to Berkeley in 1672, were one and the same.

The foregoing proves conclusively that the first state house was near the southern bank of the island and eastward of the old tower ruin.

It also seems probable that the orchard land and two houses donated to Governor Berkeley in March, 1642-43, were the same bought by the Grand Assembly from Sir John Harvey in April, 1641, and paid for in January following, and that the building previously referred to as being built by Berkeley was an addition made by him on the western side of the Harvey buildings. The westernmost of the two buildings previously owned by Harvey, therefore, became the middlemost of the block. It had been used as a courthouse in his time, as stated above, and constituted the state house during Berkeley's first term.

In the description of a tract of land patented to John Bauld-win in October, 1656, as previously noted, the land of Richard James is given as its eastern boundary, and "the slash which lyeth between the State House [land] and the said Mr. James" as its southern.[15] Richard James' land, of which patent was recorded June 5, 1657, included one hundred and fifty acres of the second ridge east of a "northerly" line passing "by" the

---

[13] *Genealogical Gleanings in England*, p. 102.
[14] *Robinson's Transcripts*, p. 258.
[15] Va. Land Pat. Records, Book IV, p. 88.

"Friggett Landing," to the marsh below "Pyping Point,"[16] including forty acres granted in 1654." The slash, forming Bauldwin's southern boundary, was the upper branch of "Pitch and Tarr Swamp," which is the northern boundary of the third and fourth ridges. The state house referred to in the patent, or probably more precisely the state house land, would seem to have been on the fourth ridge, as the part of the third ridge east of James' western line prolonged is very low ground.

During the session of the Assembly in October, 1666, an act was passed confirming the ownership of land held under unrecorded patents, on the grounds that their being unrecorded resulted from the neglect of the clerks and the destruction of the records by "two severall fires."[18] The above indicates that the repositories of the records—two state houses—had been burned prior to 1666. The "two severall fires," therefore, were doubtless those of the "old state house"—the first state house, on the southern island bank—and its successor, referred to in the Bauldwin patent, on the fourth ridge.

As Governor Berkeley sold his house in the "old state house" block to Governor Bennett, March 30, 1655, and as the Assembly passed an act during the session beginning December 1, 1656, providing for the payment of 2,500 pounds of tobacco to Thomas Woodhouse for house rent for the accommodation of the committee and for two sittings of the quarter courts,[19] held probably in June and September, 1656, preceding, it would appear that the first state house was burned between March, 1655, and June, 1656.

The second state house was probably improvised out of a private dwelling, for in those days of great inertia the four to seven months interval between the burning of the first state house and the issuing of the Bauldwin patent which contains

[16] *Ibid*, Book IV, p. 196.

[17] *Ibid*, Book III, p. 368.

[18] *Hening's Statutes*, Vol. II, p. 245.

[19] *Ibid*, Vol. I, p. 425.

the allusion to the second state house seems hardly long enough
for erecting a building.

The second state house was probably burned shortly before
1660, for during the session of the Assembly in October of that
year, house rent incurred for Assembly meetings amounting to
3,500 pounds of tobacco, and for meetings of the governor and
Council amounting to 4,000 pounds of the same medium of
exchange were appropriated and ordered paid to Thomas Hunt
and Thomas Woodhouse, respectively.[20]

During the above session Governor Berkeley was requested
by the Assembly to take charge of the building of a state house
and authorized to pay liabilities incurred therefor out of the
public funds and those to be thereafter raised by act of Assembly. He was also authorized to impress ten men to work on the
building.[21]

In 1654 a grant of an acre lot on the southern water front of
the town was made to Thomas Woodhouse.[22] Judging from the
agreement of direction of the lot's southern boundary, as given
in the patent, with the part of the river bank one hundred yards
east of the first state house, or just west of the turf fort, the lot
was near that locality. A grant of one acre on the same shore
about two hundred yards further east, was also made to Thomas
Hunt in 1655.[23] It is possible that the above tracts were those
on which were situated the taverns, in which rooms were rented
for meetings of the Assembly and for holding court. Their descriptions in the patents, however, are insufficient to definitely
locate them. Thomas Woodhouse in 1694 owned a tract on
the crest of the fourth ridge, just west of the Ambler mansion,
on which, possibly, his tavern was situated.

During a session of the Assembly in March, 1660-1661, the
expense of renting halls for holding its meetings and those of
the court was urged as a cogent reason for acquiring a state

---

[20] *Hening's Statutes*, Vol. II, p. 12.
[21] *Ibid*, Vol. II, p. 13.
[22] Va. Land Pat. Records, Book III, p. 380.
[23] *Hening's Statutes*, Vol. II, p. 32.

house, and, with a view to making the necessary taxation for the purpose as light as possible, it was resolved to solicit subscriptions. The governor, councillors, and burgesses headed the list of subscribers, donating considerable sums of money and tobacco, to be paid out of the next crop. After a lapse of over two years the matter was again brought up in the Assembly, on September 16, 1663.[24] The question as then submitted was, "Since the charge the country is yearly at for houses for the quarter courts and assemblys to sit in would in two or 3 years defray the purchase of a state house. Whether it were not more profitable to purchase for that purpose then continue for ever at the expence, accompanied with the dishonor of all our laws being made and our judgments given in alehouses."

On the day following a committee of six burgesses was appointed to confer with the governor about a state house.[25]

Under date of April 10, 1665, Thomas Ludwell, colonial secretary of state, wrote Lord Arlington that the rebuilding of the town in brick was sufficiently advanced to furnish the necessary buildings in which to transact the business of the colony. The buildings referred to by Ludwell were probably some of those erected in furtherance of the act of Assembly of December, 1662, for rebuilding the town with brick houses,[26] and it is probable that the meaning of the letter was that the state house building was completed.

There does not appear to be extant any description of the third state house. The following extract from a message addressed to the House by the governor during the session of the Assembly of 1685[27] shows that the third and fourth state house buildings occupied the same site and probably were of the same shape and proportions: "This day an addresse and some orders of yr. House have been presented to me & ye Council by some of yr. members, and doe much wonder, you should pro-

---

[24] *Ibid*, Vol. II, p. 204.
[25] *Ibid*, Vol. II, p. 205.
[26] *Ibid*, Vol. II, pp. 172, 173.
[27] *McDonald Papers*, Vol. VII, pp. 379, 380.

pose soe unreasonably, as to desire our concurrence, in ye memo-
rial [removal?] of ye secretaries office, wch. ever since ye state
House was first built, until burnt, has been continued in ye place
you allot for an office for ye Clerk, soe that Mr. Secretary justly
claims it by prescription, and you yrselves have soe consented
and alsoe desired, that it be enlarged as by ye agreement made
ye last Gen'l Assembly with Col. Ludwell." The spot, therefore, is established where, in June, 1676, Bacon, at the head of
his little army, demanded a commission to proceed against
and chastise the Indians, and where the testy old governor, while
baring his breast, reiterated the words, " here! shoot me, 'fore
God, fair mark, shoot."

After the burning of the third state house in September, 1676,
it was proposed to rebuild the town, retaining its original name,
at Tindall's Point,[28] now known as Gloucester Point, on York
River. Gloucester Point at this time was a prosperous settlement and being on salt water was probably very healthy.
" James Towne," however, was not yet to be abandoned, and in
about eight years the rebuilding of the state house on the old
site was begun.

In the interim between the burning of the third state house
and its rebuilding, the expedient of using taverns for holding
the sessions of the Grand Assembly, as had been twice done
when the colony had lost its capitol by fire, was again resorted
to, allowances of tobacco being made to Mr. Henry Gauler for
several meetings of the court and Assembly held at his tavern.[29]
In the 1685 session of the General Assembly an agreement was
entered into with Mr. William Sherwood for the use of " his
great Hall, and ye back room on ye same floor and ye cellar
under ye said room," for courthouse purposes, during the ensuing year, including " fire, candle and attendance," at twenty-
five pounds sterling per annum.[30] Sherwood's house was un-

---

[28] *Hening's Statutes*, Vol. II, p. 405.
[29] *McDonald Papers*, Vol. VII, pp. 372, 376.
[30] *Ibid*, pp. 385, 388

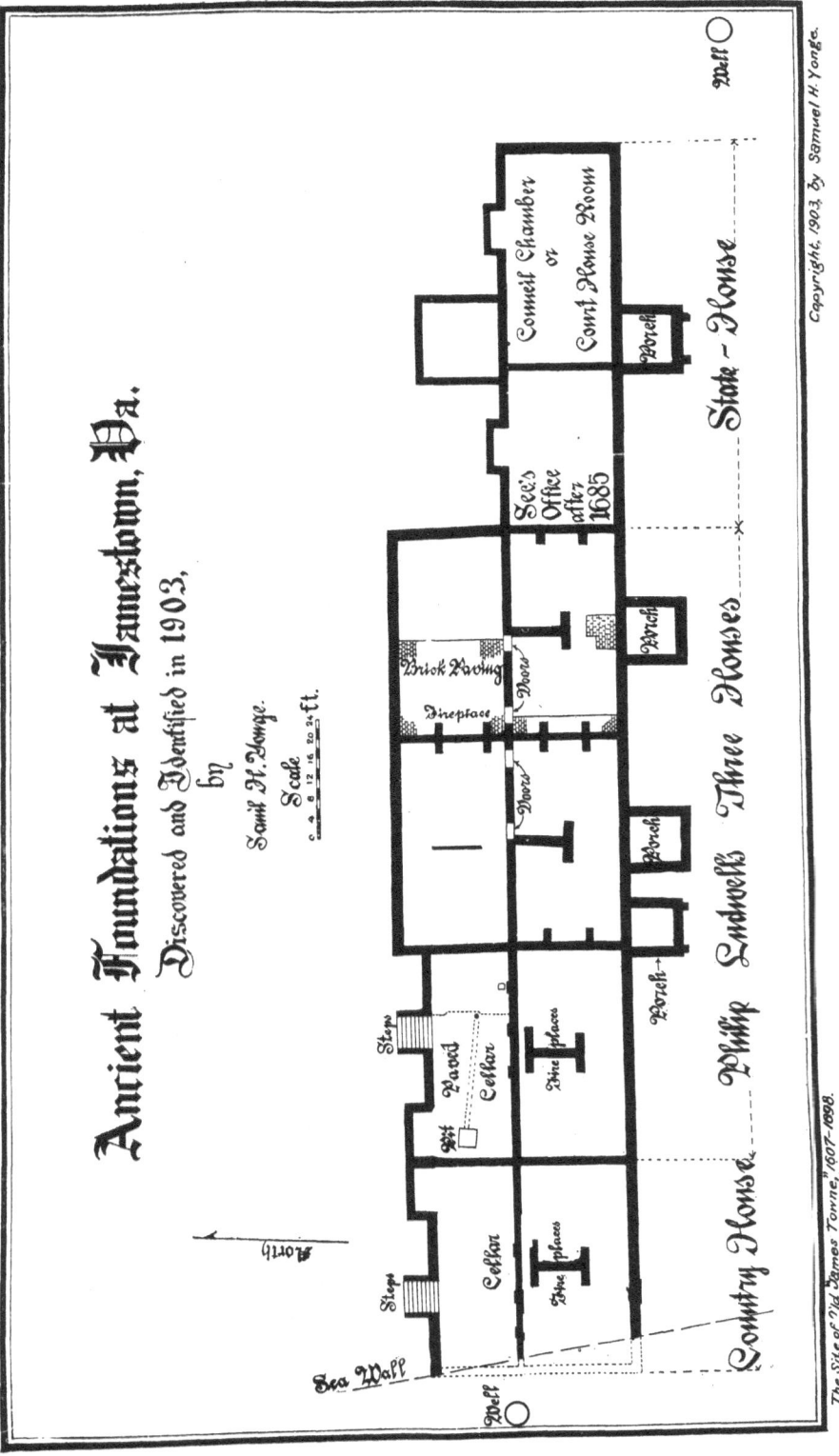

Ancient Foundations at Jamestown, Va.

Discovered and Identified in 1903,

by

Saml H. Yonge.

Scale

0 4 8 12 16 20 24 ft.

North

Steps

Yard

Cellar

Fireplaces

Well

Cellar

Three places

Fireplaces

Steps

Sea Wall

Well

Country House

Philip Ludwell's Three Houses

Porch

Porch

Porch

Brick Paving

Fireplace

Door

Doors

Sec's Office after 1685

Council Chamber or Court House Room

Porch

State - House

Well

The Site of "Old James Towne," 1607-1698.

doubtedly on the site of the acre lot bought by him in 1681, on which stood the country house.

The approximate site of the fourth state house is learned from the following quotation from a patent to William Sherwood, recorded April 20, 1694:[31] "grant unto William Sherwood of James City Gent, 308 acres of land Scituate lying and being in James City and James City Island, beginning on James River at the head of Pitch and Tarr Swamp next above the state house and running along the North side thereof" [branch of swamp]. A study of the above patent leaves no room for doubting that the branch of swamp referred to was the upper branch, from which it follows that the building stood on the third ridge.

The site of the fourth state house was unknown until early in 1903, when, as before stated, it was located by the author. A few references to its predecessor occur in " T. M.'s account of Bacon's Rebellion. This narrative, written thirty years after the above revolution, shows that the state house of 1666-1676 was a two-story building. At the eastern end of the first story was an apartment used as the council chamber and for court house purposes. In the second story was the Assembly room of the House of Burgesses, " a long room." From the manner in which the " end of the state house " is referred to by " T. M.," it might appear that the building had but one free end. This accords with the plan of the fourth state house, the western end of which, as discovered by excavating its foundations, adjoined the easternmost of Philip Ludwell's three houses referred to below.[32] The Ludwell tract had an area of one and one-half acres, in the shape of an oblong rectangle, with its northern boundary " near the Pitch and Tarr Swamp." The patent shows that the northern and southern fronts of three houses, of which the tract contained the ruins, had collectively the same length, viz., three and three-fourths chains,[33] or one hundred and

---

[31] Va. Land Pat. Records, Book VIII, p. 384.

[32] *Force's Historical Tracts*, Vol. I, p. 16.—*Bacon's Rebellion.*

[33] The chain used in the " James Citty " surveys was two poles, or thirty-three feet long.

twenty-three and three-fourths feet, and about the same azimuth as the north and south boundary lines of the tract.

In February, 1903, the earth overlying the walls found during the preceding month by probing on the crest of the third ridge where it seemed probable the ruins of the three houses mentioned in the Ludwell patent of 1694 had stood, was removed on the recommendation of the author, by the Association for the Preservation of Virginia Antiquities, when the brick foundations of a former row of buildings about two hundred and forty feet long by about twenty-four to forty-six feet wide, were disclosed at one to five feet below the surface. The foundations are on the highest part of the ridge where its elevation is about two and one-half to three and one-half feet above great tides. The ground falls gently from the foundations towards the east, and the shapes of the contours indicate that the part of the ridge abraded by the waves sloped towards the western shore.

The foundations are divided by heavy cross-walls into five principal divisions. The main walls are about two feet thick, the cross-walls from fourteen inches to two feet.

As above explained, the westernmost foundations belonged to the "Country House," those of the next three buildings to the ruins of Philip Ludwell's houses and the easternmost to the state house. All of the buildings except the state house were about forty feet square within the walls. A small proportion of the underpinning of the northernmost wall of the middle and eastern Ludwell houses is granite rubble. With the above exception the walls rest on a bed of mortar about two inches thick. On account of the base of the foundations being of different material, as above noted, and of the cross walls north of the middle main wall being out of line with those south of it, it is surmised that the northern halves of the two houses alluded to were constructed at a different period from the southern halves, possibly a later one. The inside dimensions of the earlier houses would, therefore, have been twenty by forty feet, thus according with the specifications contained in the statute of December, 1662, for rebuilding the town.

The remains of several immense fire places are found in all of the buildings excepting the state house. The fire places are generally about eight feet long between the jambs. One, in the southern half of the "Country House," is eight and a half feet long. The jambs project about three feet from the walls.

The buildings appear to have been divided into apartments about twenty feet square by the fire places and heavy partition walls.

The foundations of two of the partitions are T-shaped. It is conjectured that the spaces between the heads of the T's and the southern porches were approximately square halls, with a room at either end. The spaces between the T-heads and the middle main wall of either side of the stem of the T were probably utilized as lockers or closets. The obliquity of the T partition and also of the porch of the middle Ludwell house with reference to the main walls cannot be satisfactorily explained. It may have been the result of careless work of the builder, or it may indicate that the main walls belonged to buildings erected at different periods from the other parts referred to. The floors of two of the rooms were paved with brick, parts of the paving still remaining.

Brick foundations of several porches projecting from the southern main wall indicate that the buildings faced the south. One of the porches adjoins the middle of the state house, two others the easternmost and middle Ludwell houses. They were about ten feet square inside. Their foundation walls are eighteen to twenty-two inches thick. At the eastern end of the middle Ludwell house are what appear to have been the foundations of another and smaller porch eight and one-half feet square inside the walls. It may have belonged to a house erected prior to 1665.

Under the northern half of the westernmost Ludwell house was found a cellar, twenty by forty feet by about six feet deep, filled with the brick of fallen walls. The cellar is paved with brick. In the floor is a pit three and one-half feet square by three feet deep, with brick-lined sides. Leading from the pit to what was apparently formerly a hole about a foot in diameter is a shallow drain. It is possible that the pit was for draining the cellar, but it is far more probable that it was a well. On the floor of the cellar were several sheets of melted lead, and among the brick *débris* were a "sacar" shot, also two bombshells—one of the calibre of a demi-culverin, the other of a sacar—and fragments of exploded shells. The above warlike relics may have been fired in 1676 from Bacon's trench near the north end of the isthmus. The cellar is entered by a fight of steps on its northern side. A pipe, scissors, steel sewing-thimble, copper candle stick, ladies' riding-stirrup, and an old bottle, all of quaint and antique shapes, found in the cellar, form additions to the Association's relics.

The bond of the brick work of the cellar walls is the same as that of the foundations and tower ruin of the brick church of 1639-47—viz., the so-called English bond. This bond is found in Flanders, Holland, and Rhenish Germany, from which countries it appears to have been introduced into Great Britain.[34] Its employment at "James Towne" is probably to be accounted for by several of the residents of the town during its fourth decade being German or Dutch brickmakers and bricklayers.

"The Country House" is separated from the Ludwell buildings by an eighteen-inch party wall. Under its northern half was an unpaved cellar entered by a flight of steps on the north side similar to those of the Ludwell cellar.

The foundations of the state house show that it was about seventy-four feet by twenty feet within the walls. It was divided by a fourteen-inch cross wall into two parts, one about forty-two, the other obout thirty-one feet long. Projecting from the middle of the north wall are foundations of a wing about fifteen feet square within the walls, referred to below. On each side of the wing is a projection which may have belonged to bay win-

[34] *Encyclopedia Britannica*, Vol. IV, page 461.

SECTION OF STATE HOUSE FOUNDATIONS DISCOVERED AND EXCAVATED IN 1903

In the foreground is shown cellar of Ludwell's easternmost house, and between it and the river that of the "Country House." "The lone cypress" appears in the background.

dows or fireplaces. If not to the latter, the state house probably was not heated, as there are no other indications of fireplaces in the building.

The general plan of the state house, with its north wing and south porch, is symmetrical.

From the original transcript of the Journal of the General Assembly, held at Jamestown in May, 1684 [35] it is learned that during that session a committee consisting of " Coll° Kendall— Capt: Fra: Page—Capt: Robinson—Coll° George Mason—Mr. Hen: Hartwell—Major Allen and Mr. Sherwood," was appointed to consider the rebuilding of the state house and to ascertain its cost. The committee was also instructed to submit with its report the proposals of any persons willing to perform the work. The committee acted promptly and its report [36] was as promptly approved by the House. The report was then submitted to the governor, who appointed Mr. Sherwood to draw up a contract " between his Exlncy & the Speaker in behalfe of the Generall Assembly and the Hon[ble] Coll° Phillip Ludwell for the Rebuilding the state house."

The only available data pertaining to the arrangement of the interior of the building are the allusions to it in " T. M.'s " account of Bacon's Rebellion, and the Journal of the General Assembly held at " James Citty " in November and December, 1685 [37] quoted from above.

During the above session the rebuilding of the state house was probably nearly completed, and it was ordered by the House " That Mr. Auditor Bacon pay to Col. Philip Ludwell fower hundred pounds sterling out of ye Moneys accruing from ye duty of three pence pr. gallon upon liquors, for and in consideration of rebuilding ye State House, upon payment of wch

---

[35] Colonial Record Book, Vol. 85, pp. 168—207, P. R. O., London, England.

[36] Miss Ethel B. Sainsbury, of London, England, who examined and made transcripts of portions of the above documents for the author states that the committee's report does not appear in the files of the London P. R. O.

[37] *McDonald Papers*, Vol. VII, p. 312, *et seq.*

money, Mr. Auditor is desired to take bond from Col. Ludwell for ye full compleating of ye House, in such manner as shall be fully satisfactory to his Excellency ye Council & ye House of Burgesses answerably good and equivalent to the condition of ye same." [88]

From the same Journal of the Assembly it is learned that the Assembly room wherein the burgesses met most probably occupied the entire second floor of the main building, and that adjoining the Assembly room was a smaller apartment referred to as the porch room or porch chamber, which in the third state house had been used as the secretary's office and as a repository of the colonial records. This room, as shown by the extracts from the Assembly Journal, was a bone of contention between the governor (Lord Howard of Effingham) and the burgesses, and no doubt had much to do with the subsequent persecution of Robert Beverley, clerk of the Assembly. It is conjectured that the porch room was over the south porch.

The chamber used for the double purpose of holding sessions of the court and meetings of the Council was on the first floor—probably represented by the larger of the two divisions, the eastern, formed by the fourteen-inch cross wall. The smaller, or western, was used as a waiting-room for those having business at court. A part of the latter, at its western end, was cut off by a wooden partition in 1685 or 1686 for an office for the secretary of state. It is likely that there was a wide hall in the first story connecting the south porch and the north wing, and as "T. M." states that he saw the Council in session through the open doorway while on his way up to the Assembly, it seems likely that the hall contained the staircase.

As the foundations of the north wing are but fourteen inches thick, they probably carried walls but one story high, which prior to 1686 may have belonged to the office of the clerk of the Assembly.

---

[88] *Ibid*, p. 366.

Subjoined are extracts from the Journal of the Assembly in December, 1685, the authority for some of the foregoing deductions:

"Resolved by ye House, that ye room in ye state House, called ye Porch Chamber be kept and appropriated an office for ye Clk of ye Assbly and yt Robert Beverley [39] ye present Clerk take possession thereof and therein Lodge and place all Records, Books and Papers, belonging to ye Assembly, wch either now are or for ye time to come shall be committed to his charge keeping or Custody.

Ordered that this resolve of ye House be sent to his Excellency and ye Councel, with ye requests of this House for their concurrence therein.

Proposed by ye House, yt ye lower room in the state House opposite to ye Court House room be with all possible expidition fitted for ye Secretaries Office, And this House doe pray his Excellency will please to command and direct ye doing thereof, and yt the Honble Col Ludwell be treated with about it

Xber 4th 1685

Signed by Order of ye House of Burgesses

ROBT. BEVERLEY, Clk Assbly "

"Xber 8th 1685.

By ye House of Burgesses

To his Excellency and ye Council.

This House having read and considered yr Exclies late answer to ye resolve of this House, appointing ye room called ye Porch room in ye State House for an office for their Clerk, and that ye lower room under ye Assembly room may be fitted, soe much thereof, as is necessary, for an office for Mr. Secretary, doe now again supplicate yr Excellency and ye Council, will please to concur with them therein, for although they doe acknowledge

---

[39] Although this name is now spelled both with and without an *e* in the last syllable, the former style appears to have been that used by the above-mentioned person.

yt ye sd porch room att ye first building of ye State House was made use of for an office for ye Secretary, yet ye House of Burgesses whilst it soe remained, all along observed it, both inconvenient and incommodious to them whilst sitting; there being nothing spoken or proposed in ye House, that was not equally to be heard there, as wel as in ye Assembly room itselfe, besides ye same gave continuall opportunity to all sorts of psons to crowd before the Assembly room, under pretence of coming to ye Office.

And this House doe again propose to your Excelcy & Honrs such part of ye room, under ye Assembly rooms, as is necessary for ye Secretaries office, wch by seeling ye Walls and raising ye floor will become as safe & commodious for preservation of ye Records, as its possible any other place can be made, wch they doubt not will soe appear to yr Excellency and ye Councel, to whom they submit ye manner of doing and directions thereof, and againe request ye acceptance thereof, to that purpose.

Test   ROBERT BEVERLEY Clk Assbly.

The following answer was ordered to be returned.

By His Excellency & Council.

Your reasons given for ye Porch room to remaine an office for your Clerk, have been considered and agreed to, upon condition his Majestys Secretary upon ye first notice given him, be content that his office shall be in ye lower room you propose wch is not in ye least to be doubted, and that you will provide, that a strong partition be made under ye second girder, att ye West end of ye said room, ye floor raised two foot from ye ground, ye walls ceeled, with sawen boards smoothd and battened, and ye Windows iron barred, and shutters or Window leaves, of half inch board with a crosse barr to each, with shelves, table & benches to be well done and compleatly finished before ye next general court, att ye charge of ye Country, to be paid for ye next General Assembly, and that you agree with some workman accordingly."

It is interesting to note that Robert Beverley, who was the clerk of the Assembly in 1685, probably never occupied the porch chamber as an office, for by a letter from King James II, dated August 1, 1686, he was forever disqualified for holding office, the reason assigned for which in the letter being that he had "chiefly occasioned and promoted those disputes and contests" of the Assembly, in the stormy session of 1685. The king's letter also deprived the House of the privilege of electing its clerk, transferring to the governor authority to fill the position by appointment, and ordered Beverley's prosecution for altering the records.[40]   Beverley died shortly before April, 1687.

By an order of the General Assembly there was to be placed a "railing with rails and banisters of Locust or Cedar wood laid double in Oyle & and as close as may be ye forepart of ye State House, of convenient height & att convenient distance from ye House."[41]   The above is taken to mean that the railing was to be placed across the Assembly room to exclude spectators from the part of the hall appointed for the sessions of the burgesses.

In uncovering the foundations it was discovered that nearly all of the brick of which the walls were composed and parts of those belonging to the foundations had been removed, also some of the brick paving.

It is inferred from finding fragments of slate and tiles around the foundations that the roofs of the buildings were covered with those materials.   They were specified in the statute of December, 1662.

The row of buildings was probably completed about 1666, burned in 1676, and partly rebuilt in 1685 and 1686. The remainder of the row was possibly rebuilt between 1694 and 1698. The buildings comprising it were destroyed in the fire of October 31, 1698.

The foregoing views as to the arrangement of rooms in the fourth state house are exhibited on the accompanying plate.

---

[40] *Hening's Statutes*, Vol. III, page 41.
[41] *McDonald Papers*, Vol. VII, p. 397.

During the fall and early winter of 1903 the Association built up the foundations to the level of the ground with concrete and the walls of the cellars with the original brick. On account of the brick being very fragile the cellar walls were protected with cement plaster.

From what has preceded it is evident that the "James Citty" state houses, although substantial, were not imposing structures. In the case of the first, third and fourth, they formed part of a row or block of buildings.

It is not surprising that the colony, which a few years before the building of the fourth state house had a population of but 50,000 to 60,000 free holders,[42] could not afford out of its poverty and under its heavy burden of taxation, to have any better public buildings. The annual allowances of Culpeper as governor in 1681, alone, drained the colony of 2,150 pounds sterling,[43] which, with the perquisite of five hundred pounds sterling for house rent, reduced to present values, aggregated about $50,000.

Recurring to the Journal of the General Assembly of 1685, it contains a resolution of the House of Burgesses providing for building a prison not concurred in by the governor and Council.[44] A prison was probably erected after the completion of the fourth state house, for one was burned in the fire of October, 1698.[45]

The last meeting of the Assembly at "James Citty" was held in April, 1699, in some building unknown. At the above session an act was passed for removing the seat of government to Williamsburg. In the four succeeding years the college of William and Mary was used as a state house. In 1705 the capitol building at Williamsburg was completed. It was occupied until burned about 1747. The college was again used as a state

---

[42] *Sainsbury's Calendar of State Papers*, Vol. 1681-1685.
[43] *The Present State of Virginia*, p. 31, Hartwell, Chilton and Blair.
[44] *McDonald Papers*, Vol. VII, p. 356.
[45] *Present State of Virginia*, p. 25, Hugh Jones, A. M.

house until the capitol was rebuilt in 1755. By 1779, the centre of population having moved westward, Williamsburg was no longer well adapted as a point for assembling the legislature. For the above reason principally, and also on account of its being thought that the place was rendered unsafe by the then existing state of war, it was decided by an act of Assembly passed in the above year to transfer the seat of government to Richmond, which statute went into effect in 1780.

Arms of Captain John Smith.

THE TURF AND BRICK FORTS.

HE earliest fort of the settlers, called by them "James Forte," as previously shown, was probably situated on the river bank, at the upper extremity of the fourth ridge.

From the description of "James Citty," previously alluded to, written by the Rev. John Clayton in 1688,[1] about two years after his return to England, it appears that during his residence at "James Citty," from 1684 to 1686, there was in the town an old dismantled earth work, quadrangular in plan, "with something like Bastions at the four corners." In a grant to Henry Hartwell in 1689,[2] the western line of his tract is described as "passing along by ye angular points of ye trench which faceth two of ye Eastern Bastions of an old ruined turf fort." The above quotations undoubtedly refer to the same fort.

The Hartwell tract being accurately located, the approximate position of the fort was ascertained. According to Mr. Clayton's letter, the fort was dismantled before 1684. No mark or vestige of it remains above ground. There is apparently no information available as to when it was constructed. As the land on which it was situated was patented to Captain Ralph Hamor in 1624, the time of its construction must have been subsequent to that year, or to that of his death, 1626, on the 11th of October of which year his will was probated and his widow, Elizabeth, qualified as administratrix.[3]

It is possible that the turf fort was the one referred to by Beverley, as follows: "The news of this plot (the Birkenhead conspiracy in September, 1663), being transmitted to King Charles the second, his Majesty sent his royal commands to build a fort at James town, for security of the governor, and to

---

[1] *Force's Historical Tracts*, Vol. III.
[2] Va. Land Pat. Records, Book VII, p. 701.
[3] Transcripts Robinson MSS., p. 159.

be a curb upon all such traitorous attempts for the future. But the country, thinking all danger over, only raised a battery of some small pieces of cannon." [4]

In the account of the town by Mr. Richard Randolph in 1837 [5] it is stated in substance that some of the walls and mounds of the ancient fort still remained, that a few hundred yards to the right of the fort stood the building reputed to have been a powder magazine, and that a part of the fort had been destroyed by the encroachments of the river.

It appears from what follows that the fort referred to by Randolph was the last erected at "James Citty." The site of the former "magazine" is shown on the map.

It is assumed that, in making his observations, Mr. Randolph faced the river, the fort being down stream from, or below the magazine. If the distance between the two structures had been several hundred yards, as given by him, the site of the fort would now be in the deep water opposite the Confederate fort of 1861. This would involve an extensive change of position of the deep channel since 1837, which palpably would be impossible, for, as has been pointed out, the channel of James River at Jamestown Island is very stable, and no marked changes of its position or depth occur, even in centuries. It is, therefore, believed that Mr. Randolph meant feet, and not yards, or it is possible that the word yards is a typographic error.

The distance between the shore lines of 1837 and 1891, near the uppermost of the four jetties marked "a" on map, three hundred and twenty feet below the reputed magazine, is found approximately by using the average annual rates of abrasion of two and four feet, previously determined, to have been one hundred and ninety feet. The shore of 1891 was accurately located in that year. In 1896 it was cut back about seventy feet at the uppermost jetty to bring it to a fair line for receiving protection work. Since 1896 the recession of the bank has been very

---

[4] *History of the Present State of Virginia*, p. 56.
[5] *Southern Literary Messenger*, Vol. III, pp. 303, 304.

slight at the locality referred to. When viewed by Mr. Randolph, therefore, the shore was about two hundred and sixty feet further west than at present, and some of the mounds of the fort were then standing. At from two hundred to three hundred and fifty feet off shore, where, according to the above deductions, the fort would have stood, are what appear to be masses of masonry submerged from one and one-half to two and one-half feet below low water. The *débris* lies in what would be the extension of the "little vale" between the third and fourth ridges, from three hundred and fifty to four hundred and fifty feet to the left of the reputed magazine, with the observer facing the river, thus agreeing fairly well with Mr. Randolph's estimate of distance, amended as above suggested.

From Mr. Clayton's description of "James Citty," before referred to, it is learned that the brick fort was crescent-shaped, that a brick wall formed a part of it, probably one of its faces to retain encompassing earthworks, or mounds, as Mr. Randolph styles them, and that it was situated at the beginning of the swamp, above the town, where the channel was very near the shore.

According to Mr. Clayton also, on account of being in a vale and having its guns pointed down stream, its shot intended for an enemy's fleet would have lodged in the bank below, which was at a higher elevation than the fort, and from ten to forty yards distant. The bank which would have received the shot from the fort's guns was the former head of the fourth ridge, which formed the eastern boundary of the "little vale."

In September, 1667, an act of Assembly was passed[e] for building five forts, one of which was to be at "James Citty." Its walls were to be of brick, ten feet high, and the part facing the river ten feet thick. The fort, according to the above act, was to have an armament of eight great guns; according to another authority, it was to mount fourteen guns.[7] The above

---

[e] *Hening's Statutes*, Vol. II, pp. 255-257.
[7] *McDonald Papers*, Vol. V. p. 4.

act undoubtedly refers to the brick fort. The contractors for building the fort were Major Theophilus Hone, Colonel William Drummond, and Colonel Matthew Page. The funds for its construction do not appear to have been raised as late as September, 1672.[8] Between 1672 and 1676 a peremptory order was issued by the court requiring the surviving contractors for the fort, Hone and Drummond, to forthwith complete its construction, and providing that no further payment should be made until the work was completed.[9]

As has been shown, the channel opposite the site of the former turf fort is about twice as far from the shore as it is three hundred yards above the tower ruin, or about where the brick fort stood. This coincides with Mr. Clayton's statement that opposite the turf fort the channel was nearer the middle of the river than off the brick fort.[10]

From what has preceded it is evident that the fort referred to by Mr. Randolph was the brick fort described by Mr. Clayton, that it was situated in the extension of the depression between the third and fourth ridges, which he refers to as " a little vale," and which in fact is a minor branch of Pitch and Tarr Swamp," and that the masonry *débris* now lying under water off the uppermost of the four jetties marked " a " on chart are most probably parts of its wall, which it was proposed to make ten feet high and ten feet thick.

From Mr. Clayton's allusion to the relative positions of the brick and turf forts, with reference to that of the town, " but it is the same as if a Fort were built at Chelsea to secure London from being taken by shipping," and " There was indeed an old Fort of Earth in the town," it is apparent that in 1684 and 1686 the town, or at least the greater part of it, was below the brick fort. This agrees with available information, for at that time the only buildings known to have been standing on the third ridge were the " Country House " and the state house.

---

[8] *Hening's Statutes*, Vol. II, pp. 293, 294.

[9] Robinson's Transcripts, General Court Records, 1670-1676, p. 149.

[10] *Force's Historical Tracts*, Vol. III.

It is probable that the building reputed to have been a magazine was also standing and possibly one or two dwelling houses. There are no signs of house foundations on the ridges above the third ridge.

There appears to be no picture extant of Jamestown. In a little Dutch booklet styled the "*Scheeps-togt*" (ship's log), by Anthony Chester, Captain of the "Margaret and John," published in Holland in 1707, is an engraving of the massacre of 1622. In the clouds of the picture, mirage like, are the dim outlines of a town within a stockade. This cloud picture has been assumed by two writers to represent Jamestown in 1620 and 1622, although there is not a word in the text of the "*Scheeps-togt*" to warrant such an assumption. The picture is most probably an invention of a Dutch draftsman, made nearly a century after Chester wrote his log (1622), and who, most probably, had never been in Virginia.

"JAMES Citty," in its best days, was little more than a straggling hamlet, holding besides a church and a few unostentatious public buildings, hardly ever more than a score of dwellings, and a larger permanent population than one hundred souls. It was the foreshore on which the inrolling waves of immigration, on their way up the "Greate River," first broke. Its life, a feverish one, whose term was less than a century, terminated two centuries ago. Attempts to encourage the growth of the town by offering land bounties to those who should erect brick dwellings, as well as enactments and re-enactments making it the sole port of entry for the colony, failed signally to raise it to a place of any proportions, and after being twice lifted from its ashes, it succumbed under a third conflagration and was left prone. The town must have been held in disfavor, and avoided as a place of residence by many of the early colonists, on account of a well-earned reputation of being "insalubritious" in summer. The period of its life was not propitious for town building, as the principal efforts of the colonists were then devoted to agriculture, particularly tobacco raising.

Few relics of the old town mark its site, but its name is imperishable. Its requiem is unceasing sung in the rhythmic surgings of the "King's River."

Historical Summary of the Jamestown Period.

HE form of local government with which "the first colony," the Virginia colony, was initiated, consisted of a president and a Council of six persons. The president was elected annually by the Council out of its number. The Council also filled vacancies in its own body by elections. The methods of procedure in this body, in some respects, resembled those of a military court.

At the end of three years, the results accomplished in Virginia being unsatisfactory to the London Company, changes were made in its form of local government by abolishing the office of president and appointing instead as governor a man of high social order, and introducing a code of severe military laws. The new system was introduced on the arrival in Virginia of Sir Thomas Gates, Knight, with the title of lieutenant-governor. Of Gates and his code of laws more will be said anon.

Of the first Council, Captain Edwin Maria Wingfield, the first president, was deposed September 10, 1607, and sent home, Captain Bartholomew Gosnold, a famous navigator, "The first mover of this plantation," died within a few months after reaching Jamestown, Captain John Ratcliffe was killed by the Indians about three years later, Captain George Kendall was summarily executed in December, 1607, on account of his connection with some vaguely described "mutiny," Captain Christopher Newport died in the far East in 1617, and Captain John Smith lived to write the most complete account that we have of affairs in the early days of "Old Virginia." The remaining confrére of Smith in the first Council was Captain John Martin. At the abandonment of Jamestown by Gates in 1610, Martin alone opposed this measure. He was the founder of the Brandon estate on James River. This grant carried privileges similar to those of a lord of the manor. Being deprived of these privileges

CAPTAIN JOHN SMITH

by the first legislature in 1619, Martin became an aggressive partisan of the Smythe faction of the London Company, hereinafter referred to.

The three years under the presidents constituted a most eventful part of the Jamestown period. In its beginning, Captain John Smith, being unjustly deprived of his seat in the Council, was restored through the efforts of Rev. Robert Hunt, and within sixteen months was elected to the presidency, while those who had connived at his downfall were abased and returned to England.

Notwithstanding the fatal illness of members of the party during the first summer, by which two-thirds of its number lost their lives within three months, much was accomplished in exploring the streams of the adjacent country. Before Newport returned to England after arriving with the advance guard of the settlers, he explored James River to the "Falls," where Richmond now stands, in quest of the "Southern Sea," or of information concerning it.

As an explorer, Captain John Smith was nearly always the leader, and it was while absent on one of his expeditions, under the presidency of Ratcliffe, that Captain Kendall of the Council was implicated in the conspiracy, before alluded to.

About this time discoveries and adventures crowded rapidly on one another. Captain Smith explored the Chickahominy to its head waters, where he was captured by the Pamunkey Indians in the "slashes" of Hanover County, not far from Richmond. He was rescued from death by Pocahontas, only to be condemned by his own people immediately after his return to Jamestown, by a singular form of reprisal, to atone for the deaths of three of his party on the Chickahominy expedition. From this latter fate he was rescued by the timely arrival of Captain Newport from England with the "first supply," or reinforcement (January 4, 1608).

Next followed Newport's visit to Wahunsunacock, the Powhatan, at Werowocomico on the York River, then called the Pamunkey; then the burning of the shelter huts of the settlers in the stockade during the dead of winter. Following this disaster Newport's ship was loaded for a return voyage with clay containing mica or pyrites, under the delusion that it was gold ore. Newport and his supposed precious cargo of gold being dispatched, Smith undertook the work that made him most famous, viz., the exploration of Chesapeake Bay, which he completed in about three months. Smith's map of Virginia, based on this reconnoissance made in an open boat, often exposed to tempestuous seas, and with the crudest of instruments, was the authority for over a century. On returning from this expedition, Smith found Ratcliffe under arrest, on account of planning a desertion with the pinnace. Smith then succeeded to the presidency (September 10, 1608), and immediately after, Newport arrived with another reinforcement, called the second supply.

Shortly after Newport's arrival, the Powhatan was invited to Jamestown to be crowned, and receive as presents certain articles of apparel and household furniture. The old savage was not sufficiently complaisant to come, but demanded that the presents be brought to him. This was accordingly done, and the ludicrous farce of a forced coronation in an Indian tepee was enacted, the chief presenting Newport with his skin mantle and old shoes in return for the presents received by him. The mantle is said to be in the Ashmolean Museum at Oxford, England.

After the coronation, Newport made his second trip up the James as far as the Monacan Country, probably twenty miles above Richmond, carrying a boat in sections, all in readiness to sail on the waters of the " South Sea," or at least on a stream flowing towards it, if either should be discovered. In the second reinforcement were the first two women that came to Virginia, viz., " Mistress Forest," wife of one of the gentlemen of the party, and her maid, Anne Buras, who soon after married John Laydon, a member of the first, or original party of settlers.

Now ensued a period of great scarcity of provisions, and to make matters worse, an addition was made to the population by the arrival of the third supply (August, 1609), also scantily provided in the above respect. The newcomers were without their leader, Sir Thomas Gates, Lord La Warr's lieutenant, who had been shipwrecked in the Bermudas, and there was, for a while, as a result of his absence, much disputing as to who should be the temporary head of the colony. Some sort of order, however, was finally restored, and Smith continued, under the silent protest of the minority, to serve out his term as president. Among the last arrivals were Archer, Ratcliffe and Martin, who, while formerly living at Jamestown, had shown great animosity towards Smith. This triumvirate, in all probability, was instrumental in having Smith sent back to England in disgrace, if, indeed, this was really done, as a few writers seem to believe.

About the close of Captain Smith's presidency, Captain West, Lord La Warr's brother, who had come in the "second supply," went to the neighborhood of Richmond to establish a post, but became involved in a quarrel with the Indians, and the enterprise had to be abandoned. While returning from an inspection of this post, Captain Smith was injured by an accidental explosion of gunpowder, and lying thus wounded at Jamestown, a plot was concocted to assassinate him. This attempt failed, through the misgivings of the elected assassin. From all accounts, Smith's enemies appear to have made his life a burden, on account of which, and of his burns from the explosion, he returned to England. It is stated that charges were preferred against him. This appears very doubtful, for there is no record of his ever being brought to trial.

Smith's departure from Virginia (October 5, 1609), was followed by such serious mismanagement by Captain Percy, who was chosen to conduct the government, that within eight months, "The Starving Time," about 430 out of about 490 persons succumbed to famine and disease. At this juncture Gates, who had been cast away on the Bermudas, arrived with a slenderly provided party (May 20, 1610). Gates introduced the both famous and infamous laws, before mentioned, for the government of the colonists. These laws are plaintively described in a

petition drawn up by the so-called " ancient planters," modernly
styled old citizens, as being " written in blood." Some of the
offences which carried the death penalty were speaking im-
piously of the Trinity, derisively of Holy Writ and calumniating
the government officials. For minor offences they prescribed
milder penalties, such as branding, whipping and thrusting a
bodkin through the offender's tongue. There is record of the
last named being inflicted on a man for slandering Ralph
Hamor, secretary of state. The laws were to be read by minis-
ters to their congregations every Sunday afternoon, and worse
still, they provided for repeating a prayer by the " Captain of
the watch," both morning and evening, containing fifty per
cent. more words than all the prayers and chants of the morning
service in the Book of Common Prayer.

About two weeks after Gates' arrival he yielded to the plead-
ings of the settlers by abandoning Jamestown, being convinced
that all would starve unless this were done (June 7, 1610).
The ill and half-starved wretches embarked in their little ships
and sailed down the river on their way home. About this time
Sir Thomas West, the third Lord La Warr, the first governor of
Virginia, under the London Company, arrived at Point Comfort
and ordered the departing settlers to return, and by his words
and example, for a time, inspired the people with new courage.
Within a year La Warr was forced by ill health to leave Virginia for England (March 28, 1611).

La Warr's successor, after a short term by Captain Percy, was
Sir Thomas Dale, a heartless martinet, full of venom and vigor,
who, about the time of La Warr's departure, arrived with
" three tall ships " and three hundred men (May 19, 1611).
Dale soon established settlements at Henrico, now Dutch Gap,
and at Bermuda Hundred. He remained in the colony for
about six years, and established a reputation of a high order,
both for harshness and good management. John Smith, in a
rather docile way, censures Dale's breaking on the wheel and
racking his old and faithful sergeant, Jeffrey Abbott.

Captain Samuel Argall, than whom a more accomplished

scamp perhaps never lived, was Dale's lieutenant, and commanded the expeditions sent from Jamestown against the
French settlements in Nova Scotia, where he burned Port Royal,
settled two years before Virginia, and brought Father Biard, a
Jesuit, to Jamestown (1613). Dale would have hanged this
priest, who was an eminently good man, had it not been that
Argall, who was deeply indebted to him, interfered. With
Father Biard and his companions as prisoners at Jamestown
were two Spanish officers and a traitorous Englishman in the
service of Spain, Lymbrye by name. The three last named
prisoners were captured while reconnoitering ashore at Point
Comfort. The prison at Jamestown during Dale's administration appears to have been a vessel. Pocahontas was also at
Jamestown at this time, as a quasi prisoner, but not in close
confinement. After Captain Smith's departure she was residing with Japazaws, Chief of the Potomacs, and his wife, by
whom she was betrayed into Argall's hands for the price of a
copper kettle.

Father Biard was liberated after about nine months, and
Pocahontas was married shortly after to Rolfe. Of the two
Spaniards, one died while a prisoner, and the other, Don Diego
de Molina, a nobleman, after three years imprisonment, was
carried by Dale to England when the latter left Virginia (May,
1616). Pocahontas, Rolfe and Lymbrye were also passengers
with Dale, who, when times were dull at sea, hanged the last
named from the yard arm. Dale's ship was named the Treasurer, commanded by Captain Argall, and both ship and commander attained great notoriety as pirates.

Captain George Yeardley succeeded Sir Thomas Dale as
deputy governor, referred to by Bancroft as "mild and ineffi-
cient." During his term (May, 1616-May, 1617), Yeardley
attacked the Chickahominy Indians on account of their refusing
to furnish him with corn, according to a previous understanding
with Dale, and also on account of their assuming a threatening
attitude when Yeardley went to collect the corn from them.
According to some accounts, Yeardley's above action was un-

justifiable, and it was stated by those who were unfriendly to him to have been a cause of the massacre of the colonists which occurred six years later.

In March, 1617, Pocahontas died at Gravesend in England, and Rolfe returned to Virginia, leaving his son Thomas with Sir Lewis Stukeley at Plymouth. After serving as governor for about a year, Captain Yeardley was relieved by Captain Samuel Argall as deputy governor to Lord La Warr. Argall left the colony clandestinely after about two years of misrule, and in less than a fortnight Yeardley, recently knighted, returned with the title of Governor and Captain General, as successor to Lord La Warr, who had died in 1618, while on his way to Virginia. Captain Nathaniel Powell was deputy governor during the ten days interval between the departure of Argall and the arrival of Yeardley.

The affairs of the Virginia colony had now been under the direction of Sir Thomas Smythe, treasurer or manager of the London Company, for about twelve years, during the greater part of which time more or less dissatisfaction was expressed with the management, on account of unremunerative results. Sir Thomas was a wealthy merchant, and took a leading part in most of the great enterprises of the day for extending commerce into distant lands. He was one of the founders of the scheme for discovering the Northwest Passage. In consequence of Argall's maladministration, despotic methods and dishonest acts while in the above office, Sir Thomas Smythe was severely censured by Sir Edwin Sandys and Sir Henry Wriothesley, Earl of Southampton, leaders of one of the factions into which the Company had become divided on account of petty jealousies and differences of opinion as to its policies.

Both Sandys and Wriothesley were men of the highest character. Sandys was one of the framers of the remonstrance addressed to King James on account of his treatment of his first Parliament. Wriothesley was a courageous man, who seldom hesitated to boldly assert his convictions. He was an intimate

THOMAS LaWARR, Third Baron Delaware
First Governor of Virginia, under the London Company

of Sandys, who, it is stated, converted him to the reformed faith.

Sandys was the leader of the " independent party " in Parliament, which opposed the Royal prerogative against " the rights of the Parliament and the liberty of the subject," and on account of his activity and zeal, in advocating this principle in Parliament, was, with other members, imprisoned. Thus did King James sow the wind of which Prince Charles was to reap the whirlwind.

At an election for treasurer of the Company held in April, 1619, Sir Thomas Smythe refused re-election, and the candidates placed in nomination by his faction, that of the merchants, were defeated by Sir Edwin Sandys, an advocate of a popular form of government in Virginia. The election of Sandys greatly angered the king, who recognized in it the influence in the London Company of those who in Parliament were opposed to his policies. At the election for treasurer in the following year the king forbade the nomination of Sandys, and proposed for the office the names of Smythe and three of his adherents. The company resented this invasion of its charter rights by electing by vociferous acclamation, to the office of treasurer, Sir Henry Wriothesley, " The friend of Shakespeare." On account of Wriothesley's election the king became still more incensed against the Company, and at once set about to accomplish its downfall. Wriothesley was re-elected treasurer during the succeeding four years of the Company's existence.

To further his plans for overthrowing the Company, the king called to his service Sir Samuel Argall, whom he knighted in June, 1622. He also summoned for the same purpose Nathaniel Butler, erstwhile governor of the Bermudas, who, on account of malfeasance in office, had fled to Virginia, where during his three months sojourn in 1622 he perpetrated several high-handed acts, among them that of stealing Dame Dale's cows. Dame Dale was the relict of Sir Thomas, and at that time resided in the suburbs of Jamestown.

On Butler's return to England he published, at the instance

of the king, "The Unmasked Face of our Colony in Virginia as it was in the Winter of 1622." In this paper Butler attacked the management of colonial affairs under Sandys and Southampton,. and defended the administration of Sir Thomas Smythe. Butler's charges were replied to in an equally quaint and curious document styled "The denial of Nathaniel Butler's the Unmasked Face," etc. It was subscribed to by twenty-four persons, including Sir Francis Wyatt, Governor, the members of Wyatt's Council and members of the Assembly. Another paper of similar import to "The Unmasked Face," bearing the title of "The Alderman's Declaration," emanating from Alderman Johnson, who had been Sir Thomas Smythe's deputy while he was treasurer, was also answered by practically the same persons who had replied to Butler's screed.

The following extracts from Stith's rendition of the answer to "The Alderman's Declaration" and from "The denial of Nathaniel Butler's 'The unmasked Face,'" furnish a pathetic epitome of the tragedy of the early settlement:

From the answer to the "Alderman's Declaration:"—"That in those twelve years of Sir Thomas Smith's government the colony for the most part remained in great want and misery & under most severe and cruel laws, which were sent over in print, and that the allowance of a man in those times was only eight ounces of meal and half a pint of pease a day, both the one and the other being moldy, rotten, full of cob webs and maggots, loathsome to man and not fit for beasts which forced many to fly to the savage Enemy in relief who being again taken were put to sundry kinds of death by hanging, shooting, breaking upon the wheel and the like. That others were forced by famine to filch for their bellies of whom one for stealing three pints of oatmeal had a bodkin thrust thro his tongue and was chained to a tree till he starved. That if a man thro' sickness had not been able to work he had no allowance at all and so perished. That many through these extremities dug holes in the Earth and there hid themselves till they famished. * * That the scarcity sometimes was so lamentable that they were constrained to eat dogs, cats, rats, snakes, toadstools, horse-hides, and what not. That one man out of the misery he endured killed his wife and powdered her up to eat for which he was burnt, that many others fed upon the corpses of dead men and that one who through custom had got an insatiable appetite for that food could not be restrained till he was executed for it and that indeed so miserable was their state that the happiest day many ever hoped to see was when the Indians killed a mare, the people wishing as she was boiling that Sir Thomas Smith was on her back in the kettle."

From the " denial " to Nathaniel Butler's " The unmasked Face :" " His computation of 10,000 souls falleth short of 4,000 & those were in great part wasted by the more than Egyptian slavery and Scythian cruelty which was exercised on us your poore and miserable subjects by Laws written in blood and executed with all kinds of Tyranny in the time of Sir Thomas Smith's government, whereof we send your Majesty the true and Tragical Relation."

It is to be inferred from these acrimonious writings that the material condition of the settlers could not have been much worse under one administration than the other; also that under the Smythe régime this condition resulted, in a large measure, from perfunctoriness, indifference and bad management, while under Sandys and Southampton the last named was the sole cause.

It is generally understood that on account of the assistance rendered by Butler in furthering the king's efforts to destroy the Company, the charges of mal-administration against him were suppressed.

In the spring of 1623 a formal complaint was lodged with the Privy Council and Lord Treasurer against the Company. This was ably answered and the charges refuted by Sandys, Cavendish and Ferrar, who, for their pains, were placed under duress. The king then appointed a commission to investigate affairs in Virginia, including Sir Samuel Argall, Captain John Harvey, John Pory, Abraham Peirsey and Samuel Matthews. The commissioners found in the local Virginia government warm supporters of the Sandys and Southampton administra-

8—J. T.

tions. In the summer of 1623 the attorney general rendered an opinion advising that the government of Virginia be transferred to the king. The company was called on to surrender its charter. This order Sandys and his associates declined to obey. A petition from the Company to Parliament to consider the rights of the Company was met by the king's order to forbear, and the petition was tabled. *Quo warranto* proceedings followed. In presenting the case for the Crown the attorney general held that the power conferred on the Company by the charter in respect to immigration was too great, and that by its exercise the depopulating of Great Britain might result, by all of its people being transferred to America. This argument was considered irrefutable by the lord chief justice, and on June 16, 1624, the Company's charter was annulled.

An attempt was made to re-establish the Company about fourteen years later, but King Charles assured the remonstrating colonists that this would not be done.

Yeardley was appointed governor towards the close of the Smythe régime, but owed his appointment to the influence of the Sandys faction. He appears to have been especially selected to succeed La Warr on account of his aptitude for carrying out the Sandys policy of a popular form of government. He served for upwards of two years (April 19, 1619-November 18, 1621). His term was made famous by three incidents, viz., the convening of the first legislative body in America (July 30, 1619), the arrivals of young women sent to Virginia to become wives of the settlers, and the arrival of the first African slaves (August, 1619). The Assembly met at this time in the little frame church fifty feet by twenty feet in plan, built in Argall's term, and previously referred to, and the pomp and ceremony with which the meetings were conducted must have contrasted strangely with the simplicity and rudeness of this little edifice.

Sir Francis Wyatt, Knight, succeeded Yeardley. He was a man of education, but apparently not a soldier. About this time (May 28, 1621) the opinion was expressed by a Virginia divine, Parson Stockton, that " till their [the Indian's] Priests

SIR HENRY WRIOTHESLEY
Third Earl of Southampton
Third and last Treasurer of the London Company

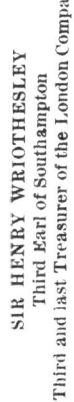

SIR EDWIN SANDYS
Second Treasurer of the London Company

and Ancients have their throats cut, there is no hope to bring them to conversion." This heroic treatment, while only suggested by the clergyman, in despair of bettering the spiritual condition of the savages, was adopted by the latter in the massacre on March 22 (Good Friday), 1622, of the unsuspecting and confiding settlers.

Wyatt remained in Virginia as governor for about six years, and was joined by Lady Wyatt in the second year of his term, or about a year after the first massacre.

Notwithstanding the improved condition of the colonists, compared with that previously existing, Lady Wyatt, writing to her sister in England, states that the ship in which she crossed the Atlantic was "so pestered with people and goods, so full of infection, that after a while they saw little but throwing folks overboard." On land she found little to encourage her, and would be undone unless her sister or mother could help her. Butter, bacon, cheese and malt were especially needed.

In the year of the massacre and that following, there was a great influx of immigrants, inadequately provided with subsistence stores. On account of the hostility of the Indians and the abandoning of farms after the massacre, very little maize was planted and harvested. George Sandys, treasurer, uncle of Lady Wyatt, in writing home states that "the living could hardly bury the dead;" also that the beer furnished by a contractor named Dupper had "poisoned most of the passengers on shipboard, and had spread the infection all over the colony;" evidently referring to an epidemic of some kind unstated, possibly cholera.

During Wyatt's first term occurred one of the most important events in the colony's history, viz., the formal granting of a constitution providing for a civil form of government, of which the convening of the legislature about two years before by Yeardley was the forerunner.

On the retiring of Sir Francis Wyatt from office, Sir George Yeardley began his second term as governor (May, 1626), which was terminated in about six months by his death on November 27, 1627. His father was a merchant tailor of London. Sir George served with distinction against the Spaniards, in the Netherlands, and came to Virginia seventeen years before his death as captain of Lieutenant Governor Gates' company. He owned an estate at Flowerdew[1] Hundred on James River, and another in Accomac County on the "Eastern Shore." He is criticised by one writer for making a great parade in London after he was knighted, and the poet George Sandys, in a letter to England, relates that he was "too much taken up with his own affairs." With his name are associated the most pleasing memories of "James Towne."

According to Yeardley's second commission, Captain John Harvey was to succeed him in event of his death, and Captain Francis West, brother of Lord La Warr, was named as successor to Harvey. The latter being in the naval service under Buckingham, West was duly installed in the office, which he filled for about sixteen months. At this time the immigration to Virginia was very large.

Dr. John Pott was elected by the Council to act as governor on March 5, 1629, during Captain West's absence in England, and held the position till the arrival of the new governor and captain-general, Sir John Harvey (March 24, 1630). The hypercritical George Sandys, the poet, refers to Dr. Pott, in one of his letters from Jamestown, as "a pitiful councillor," and in another as "a cipher."

A notable act of the Assembly approved by Governor Pott provided for attacking the Indians at intervals of four months, and another restricted the quantity of tobacco to be planted by each person.

Several months after Dr. Pott was relieved by Sir John Harvey he was convicted of appropriating other people's cattle, but sentence was withheld till the matter could be submitted to the king. In the meanwhile, the members of the Council became

---

[1] Professor Arber suggests that the intended name was Florida Hundred.

the ex-governor's bondsmen, and Mrs Pott hurried across the Atlantic and personally appealed to King Charles I, who finding the evidence insufficient, granted the pardon.

Governor Harvey was one of the commissioners sent by King James I to Virginia, prior to the annulling of the London Company's charter in 1623, to report on the condition of the colony. He at that time patented a tract of land on the south bank of the James River, about five-eighths mile below the present wharf (see map). While Sir John was governor, he lived, according to some accounts, in considerable style. A former fellow sea captain named De Vries tells of Harvey's meeting him at the wharf with an escort of halberdiers and musqueteers and of entertaining him right royally at his Jamestown home.

Sir John incurred the dislike of his Council by his friendly attitude towards the forming of Lord Baltimore's colony of Maryland out of northern Virginia. Dislike was ripened into open hostility by the governor's contumacious conduct, and culminated in open revolt when he intercepted the councillors' letters to the king. He was finally deposed and sent back to England (April 28, 1635). King Charles disapproved of the Council's course in deposing Harvey, and within two years sent him back to Virginia to resume the office of governor. He relieved Captain John West January 18, 1637, who had been elected acting governor by the Council.

About the time of Harvey's deposal occurred the famous little battle between citizens of Virginia and Maryland, whose diminutive navies were respectively commanded by Ratcliff Warner and Councillor Thomas Cornwallis. The question at issue was, to which of the above colonies Kent Island belonged.

The immigration to Virginia was larger during Harvey's administration than ever before. Nearly all of these immigrants were indentured servants. The building of brick houses was begun, and the first possessor of one, Richard Kemp, wrote about this time that there was " Scarce any but hath his garden and orchard." Kemp's house, according to my investigations, was slightly east of the dwelling house built after the War between the States on the site of the former Ambler-Jaquelin mansion, burned during that war. No more striking proof could be afforded of the simple life of the Jamestonians of that time, a full generation after the first settlement was made, than the pride which they displayed over the acquiring of the first brick house, only sixteen by twenty-four feet.

The establishment of the first free institution of learning in the New World by the bequest of Benjamin Symms in 1635, antedated the endowment by John Harvard of the university that bears his name. Symms' school was situated in Elizabeth City Parish, Virginia, not far from Point Comfort.

This was not the first effort made in Virginia in behalf of education. Fifteen years earlier fifteen hundred pounds sterling had been raised by the English bishops at the instance of King James the First for erecting a college for educating the Indians, and a single contribution of five hundred and fifty pounds sterling was made for the same purpose in 1622. The scheme of educating the Indians seems to have been abandoned after the massacre of 1622.

At the expiration of Harvey's second term (November, 1639), he was reduced almost to beggary by judgments obtained against him by those whom he had defrauded during his administrations.

Sir Francis Wyatt succeeded Harvey, and held the office of governor for one and one-half years (February, 1642).

Richard Kemp was secretary of state under Sir Francis Wyatt, and was accused of secretly leaving Virginia and carrying away the charter and records of the colony. He subsequently returned and filled his former office under the successor of Wyatt, Sir William Berkeley.

In Bruton Parish Churchyard near the door of the north transept of the church is a tomb placed by Philip Ludwell, bearing an epitaph to his uncle, Thomas Ludwell, Sir Thomas Lunsford, Knight, and Richard Kemp, the two last named being buried elsewhere in the churchyard.

The annals of Jamestown of the time of Sir William Berkeley's administrations are full of interest. Sir William is probably oftener referred to than any other colonial governor. He took his degree at Oxford at the age of nineteen, and subsequently traveled extensively on the continent. He was a versatile man, and among his achievements wrote a play, " The Lost Lady," which Pepys notes in his diary having seen performed in London. When he came to Virginia in 1642, he displayed great zeal in performing his duties, and manifested a deep interest in the welfare of the people and extreme loyalty to the sovereign. In his later years he was irascible, covetous and despotic.

Sir William was a perfervid Royalist, and a man of great ambitions. He was a staunch supporter of the State Church and enforced the laws excluding those of other sects from Virginia. His failure to amass great wealth and attain advancement after spending thirty-four years in Virginia, coupled with poor health, probably accounts, in a large measure, for the petulant and overbearing disposition for which he was noted in the closing years of a career which began so auspiciously, and terminated so ignominiously.

Sir William married about his sixtieth year, in 1670, Frances Culpeper, the widow of ex-Governor Stephens, of North Carolina, and left no descendants.

Sir William served two terms as governor of Virginia, the first of about ten (February, 1642-April 30, 1652), the second of about seventeen years (March 13, 1660-April 27, 1677). The second Indian massacre, led, as was the first, by Opechancanough, brother and successor to the Sachem Wahunsunacock, commonly known as Powhatan, occurred (April 17, 1644) on " Holy Thursday," near the end of the second year of Governor Berkeley's first term. In it about three hundred of the settlers were mui dered.

About this time Sir William visited England for consultation with the Royal government. The trip was made necessary by the outbreak of the Revolution. Shortly after his return to Virginia in June, 1645, he attacked Opechancanough's force

and captured the old blind chief, who, while confined at Jamestown, was treacherously murdered by his jailers.

Richard Kemp, president of the Council, acted as governor
during Sir William's absence of about one year. Under Kemp's
administration laws were passed by the Assembly intended to
diminish the consumption of spiritous liquors by imposing a
heavy tax on their sale.

During Sir William's first term the colony prospered, and its
population increased. While the Revolution in England was in
progress, notwithstanding a division of sentiment in the colony
as to the burning issue of the times, Cromwell versus Royalty,
matters proceeded harmoniously. Among Cromwell's adherents
in Virginia were several prominent persons, including Captain
Stegge, Richard Bennett, William Claiborne and Samuel
Matthews.

When Sir Wiliam Berkeley was relieved of office under the
Commonwealth, Richard Bennett was elected his successor by
the Grand Assembly. Bennett served for about three years
(April 30, 1652-March 31, 1655). He was a Puritan elder,
and on account of his religious views had been obliged to leave
Virginia during Berkeley's first term (1648). From Virginia
he went to Maryland, thence to England. In September, 1651,
he was appointed a member of the commission nominated by
Parliament to receive the surrender of the colonies, of which the
other members were William Claiborne, Edmund Curtis, Robert
Dennis and Thomas Stegge.

Governor Bennett was succeeded by Edward Digges, who
served about three years (March 31, 1655-March 13, 1658).
An important event of his term was the defeat of the colonial
forces and their Indian allies, the Pamunkeys, under their chief
Tottopottomoy, under the command of Colonel Edward Hill, at
Bloody Run, near Richmond, Va., by the Richicrechian Indians.

Governor Digges' successor was Captain Samuel Matthews
(March 13, 1658-January, 1660). Captain Matthews was one
of the councillors who, as before mentioned, " thrust out of his
government " Sir John Harvey.

During the session of the Assembly in which Matthews was elected governor, a resolution was adopted to exclude the governor and Council from the sessions of the House of Burgesses. The governor unsuccessfully opposed the measure.

The policy of Cromwell towards Virginia was far more pacific and liberal than that under Royal rule, either before or after the interregnum. In consequence, the country duly prospered under the Commonwealth. The three Roundhead governors, Bennett, Digges and Matthews, were excellent and worthy men.

Under the terms of surrender to the Parliamentary Commissioners, Virginia was to enjoy all of her ancient privileges, and be free from all taxes and customs except such as were imposed by its own legislature.

On the death of " worthy Captain Matthews," the last Roundhead governor, about six weeks before the Restoration, Sir William Berkeley was elected by the Assembly to his second term. Now the ingratitude and selfishness of the Stuarts was made conspicuous by the conduct of Charles the Second towards Virginia, for instead of being at least as considerate as Cromwell, he rewarded his ever faithful subjects by imposing heavier taxes on them than they had ever before experienced.

The oppressive taxes were carried by the Navigation Act, passed by the Rump Parliament in 1653. By this act, as amended under King Charles II, all trade by the colonists was to be carried on exclusively with British subjects in England, in English or colonial built vessels, commanded by English officers, and manned by a crew of which at least 75 per cent. were to be Englishmen.

The penalties for infractions of the law were extremely severe. The English merchants thus became monopolists, fixing the prices of both the products received from Virginia and the commodities which they sent there. The colonists, however, still enjoyed free trade with the neighboring colonies. After suffering for nine years under this oppressive measure, their burden was made still more onerous by the subjecting of local

trade with New Amsterdam and New England to the same taxes
as trade with the Mother Country. In consequence of the Navigation Act, the colonists were impoverished, and a spirit of dissatisfaction and unrest was created. Notwithstanding the
impoverishment and suffering wrought by the act, the colony
would probably have escaped the revolution known as Bacon's
Rebellion, had it not been for Berkeley's unjust and impolitic
course in perpetuating the same Assembly for sixteen years by
successive prorogations, instead of ordering, according to custom, elections for new Assemblies, and by failing to punish the
aggressions of the Indians for fear of thereby incurring personal
losses in the fur trade.

About four months after Sir William's election, Charles the
Second was proclaimed king. In April, 1661, Sir William went
to England on official business and left Colonel Francis Moryson
to act as governor till his return in the fall of 1662. Making
due allowance for the narrow mindedness of the age, Colonel
Moryson appears to have been a man with some liberal ideas.

In 1667, and again in 1673, Dutch fleets appeared at the
mouth of James River and destroyed the English shipping.

In the summer of 1675, certain Susquehanna Indians who
had been driven south by the warlike Senecas, and had lodged
with the Piscataquas at the head of Chesapeake Bay, crossed the
Potomac into Virginia and stole some swine. The marauders
were pursued into Maryland by the Virginians, led by Colonel
George Mason and Major George Brent, and, in the pursuit,
several friendly Susquehannas and a chief were killed. Re-
prisals followed by the Indians, who quickly gathered into one
of their towns which they fortified.

A large body of Marylanders and Virginians under the leader-
ship of the above officers and Colonel John Washington appearing before the town, five Indian chiefs came out for a parley.
These, it would appear, were slain, without provocation. The
town was then beseiged for about seven weeks, when the entire
body of Indians unexpectedly made a night sally and escaped.

The only measure which had thus far been provided by the

colonial government for protecting the frontiers against the Indians was the establishing at remote points of a few insignificant forts. These posts, on account of being so widely separated, afforded no security to the settlers, while their maintenance was a great drain on the public purse, which caused general dissatisfaction.

In January, 1676, a band of Susquehannas attacked the frontier settlements at the heads of the Virginia rivers, and slew many of the settlers. Governor Berkeley ordered a force to be assembled by Sir Henry Chicheley to punish the Indians. Before the order was carried out, however, the troops were disbanded without making any demonstration. The governor's reprehensible conduct in this matter, by which an extensive area of sparsely peopled country was exposed to the depredations of the savages greatly incensed the people, and it became common talk among the gossips that " no bullets could pierce bever skins." In response to a petition from the people for an organized force to proceed against the Indians, the governor forbade the presenting of any further such petitions, under severe penalties. This caused some to naively remark that " rebbell forfeitures would be royal inheritances."

News of an invasion by the Indians being received, a large gathering of the people of the upper tidewater counties was held, at which Nathaniel Bacon, Jr., of Curle's Neck, was prevailed on to take command of a band of three hundred volunteers, for which position the governor was requested to grant him a commission.

Bacon was an educated man, of good family. He came to Virginia when about thirty years of age, with his wife Elizabeth Duke, about 1674, and settled at Curle's Neck, about twenty miles below Richmond. He was of an impulsive and impetuous nature, and a born leader of men. He left two daughters, but no sons.[2]

---

[2] Colonel Gordon McCabe, in Times-Dispatch, Richmond, Va., Jan. 12, 1907.

The commission not being forthcoming, Bacon set out without one, and attacked and killed a number of Ockinagee Indians, to whom he had applied for subsistence for his men, but who gave in return, possibly at the instigation of the governor, only evasive replies. These Indians were regarded as friendly.

The governor at once proclaimed Bacon and his followers as being in a state of rebellion, ordered them to disband, and set out with a small party to intercept them. Failing in this, and probably being aware of the murmurings of dissatisfaction of the people at his shortcomings, he at once, on his return to Jamestown, ordered an election to be held for new burgesses, and directed a number of the useless and expensive forts to be abandoned.

Nathaniel Bacon, Jr., who had heretofore been a member of the Council, was nominated as a burgess from Henrico County, and being duly elected, proceeded in June, 1676, to the capital, to take his seat in the Assembly. Being apprised, on his arrival near the town, of the governor's intention to arrest him, he attempted to return up the James. His sloop, however, was overtaken, and he and a number of his adherents were arrested and taken before the governor.

The crafty Berkeley, mindful that Bacon's influence could be more effectually curtailed by keeping him out of the Assembly, restored him to the Council. This, however, was not done until, at the instance, and under the persuasion of his kinsman, Colonel Nathaniel Bacon, Sr., Bacon had acknowledged his transgression and besought the governor's pardon in a " parasiticall " paper formally presented on bended knee.

Immediately following Bacon's pardon and restoration to the Council, the Assembly declared war against the Indians, and nominated Bacon as commander of the forces to be employed against them. The governor acquiesced in Bacon's appointment, and promised to issue a commission to him within a few days. After vainly waiting several days for the commission, Bacon returned to his home at Curle's Neck, on James River.

It is stated by some that Bacon obtained the governor's permission to leave Jamestown under the plea of his wife's illness, also that he had been warned to seek safety in flight from the governor's hostility. It is probable, however, that Bacon, being a man of great perspicuity and determination, was aware of the governor's insincerity, and would not brook temporizing.

On June 21, at "2 of the clock," within a week of Bacon's departure, he returned to Jamestown, crossed the isthmus and invaded the island at the head of four to five hundred armed men. Bacon's entrance was entirely unopposed. His troops formed on a green "not a flight shot distant," or less than one hundred yards, from the state house on the third ridge.

In a half hour the burgesses were assembled by drum beat, and in an hour Bacon proceeded to the state house with a guard of fusileers. Near the corner at the eastern end of the building he was met by the governor and Council. Both of the principals to the meeting were greatly excited, the governor baring his breast and challenging Bacon to shoot him, while the latter reassuringly replied that the procuring of a commission to fight the Indians, and not the infliction of personal injury on the governor, was his only purpose. In the meanwhile, the fusileers of Bacon's guard intimidated the burgesses gazing at this exciting scene from the upper story of the state house, by leveling their pieces with matches lighted at the windows, and vociferously demanding their leader's commission. It is also reported that Bacon muttered "Dam my blood, I'll kill governor and Council, Assembly and all, and then I'll sheathe my sword in my own heart's blood," and that all that was necessary to carry this blood-curdling vow into execution was the drawing of his sword, which was prevented by the "waiving of a pacifick hankercher" by one of the aforesaid burgesses, accompanied by assurances that the commission would be given him.

The following day a commission was presented to Bacon, who promptly rejected it, probably on the score of its insufficiency, and another was soon drawn which met his approval. After passing an act carrying full pardon to Bacon and his followers for their previous unauthorized and illegal acts during the uprising, the Assembly adjourned.

General Bacon at once started for the appointed rendezvous of his forces at the Falls of James River, and the governor skulked to Gloucester.

Reassured by the recent action of the governor and Assembly, the people rallied to Bacon's standard.

On the very eve of Bacon's departure to attack the Indians, news was brought to his army that Governor Berkeley had again proclaimed him a rebel, and had called out the Gloucester militia to march against him. The people, however, were lukewarm, five-sixths of them, it is said, being in sympathy with Bacon. The militia, therefore, did not respond to the governor's call. Learning of Bacon's being on his way to Gloucester, the governor left for Accomac across Chesapeake Bay.

Bacon then made Middle Plantation (midway between Jamestown and Yorktown; later Williamsburg) his headquarters, and issued a proclamation declaring the governor and Council traitors, and requiring their apprehension and surrender. He also summoned the leading men of the colony to his camp to advise on the colony's affairs. After calling a meeting of the Assembly for September 4, and sending an armed vessel under Giles Bland and Richard Carver to capture Berkeley at Accomac, Bacon again sallied forth against the Indians. In the marshes of York River he was joined by Colonel Brent with four hundred men, who ostensibly had gone out to oppose him. The united forces scoured the country, and drove the Pamunkey Indians from their fastnesses.

Bacon's naval expedition ended disastrously, both commanders and vessel being captured by a ruse. A writer of the time states that the capture was "caused by their indiscretion and the juice of the grape." Bland was taken by an old enemy, Philip Ludwell, whose brother Thomas, secretary of state, he had challenged by nailing his glove against the secretary's door.

The governor having raised a force of six hundred men, left Accomac for Jamestown with fifteen sail and, appearing before the town September 7, demanded its surrender. The seven hundred raw recruits under Colonel Hansford at once withdrew, and Sir William entered the town, the old hypocrite falling on his knees to offer thanks for his return. On learning of the governor's movements, Bacon hurried, by a forced march, to Jamestown, arriving at the isthmus with about three hundred footsore and tired men.

Over night, a work of earth and fascines was thrown up by Bacon's men on which, the following day, the guns of Sir William's vessels opened an ineffective fire. While the firing was in progress Bacon extended his work and shortly after received and repulsed a half-hearted assault of Berkeley's men.

Bacon having brought up " two great guns," " The one he sets to worke ('playing some calls it that takes delight to see stately structures beated down and men blown up in the air like shuttle cocks ')," the other to breach Berkeley's work on Block House Hill, at the southern end of the isthmus (see map). It appears that while moving these guns over the rough ground and emplacing them, Bacon exposed the wives of the members of Sir William's Council, whom he had taken into custody for the purpose, as a shield for his working party. This act would make Bacon appear rather more resourceful than gallant.

It was now Berkeley's turn to evacuate the town. Disheartened by the failure of his attack on Bacon, and yielding to the importunities of his men, he embarked his forces, under cover of night, and dropped down the James. The next morning Bacon entered the town and " that the wolves might harbour there no more " burned it the same night.

From near Mulberry Island, made memorable as the point where, over sixty years before, Captain Brewster met Gates with La Warr's instructions to return with his party to Jamestown, which they had just deserted, Sir William's party viewed the glare of the flames consuming the product of years of toil and suffering.

Bacon's next move was to Green Spring, from which he issued a manifesto against the governor. He then marched to Gloucester, where the seeds of disease planted by exposure developed into dysentery, from which he died. His burial place was kept secret to prevent his body being disinterred and hung in chains, and has never been revealed.

Thus died the people's champion, but not in vain. His example in resisting tyranny and oppression survives, and his cause, which seemingly was lost really conquered in its defeat.

· After Bacon's death his party quickly fell to pieces for want of a leader, and by January 16, 1677, about seven months after its inception, the revolution was at an end.

The execution of twenty-three of his prisoners by Sir William Berkeley brought obloquy upon his name from both king and people. The hapless victims of the governor's wrath, after passing through the mockery of drum-head courts-martial, were strung up usually wherever they were tried or where it would best suit the governor's whim. These executions were made under a proclamation issued by Berkeley, who suppressed the king's proclamation, which excepted from pardon only Nathaniel Bacon, Jr.

The wave of revolt had scarcely passed before a wholesale confiscation was begun by the governor, who placed "the broad arrow" on property of all kinds, including the belongings of those whom he had widowed and orphaned by his bloody executions. Some of this property was appropriated to his own uses, and formed the bases of suits against Lady Berkeley for several years after Sir William's death.

Sir William was as loath to leave Virginia as his successor, Thomas, Lord Culpeper, was to go there. He disregarded the king's recall made in November, 1676, and did not leave Virginia until May, 1677, after the king's summons had been repeated.

Lady Berkeley wielded great influence over her husband and his supporters, and after Sir William's departure from Virginia, was the head of a cabal which intrigued against Colonel Jeffreys, the lieutenant-governor. The other members of this cabal were Colonel Philip Ludwell, Colonel Thomas Ballard,

Colonel Edward Hill and Major Robert Beverley.[*] Lady
Berkeley was apparently very proud of the title of courtesy
acquired by her marriage with Sir William, for, contrary to
custom, she used it after her marriage to Colonel Ludwell, and
it is to be seen on the only remaining fragment of her tombstone
in the Jamestown churchyard.

Sir William's immediate successor was Colonel Herbert
Jeffreys. one of the three commissioners sent to Virginia in the
autumn of 1676 to report on Bacon's Rebellion. He commanded
the regiment then sent to Virginia from England, " His Majestie's own regiment of Foot," the First Grenadier Guards. He was
directed to conduct affairs till Lord Culpeper should arrive.

Culpeper, with other noblemen, favorites of King Charles the
Second, had been granted the Northern Neck, or Potomac Neck,
in 1669, and in 1673 received a grant of the entire colony for a
term of thirty-one years. He was appointed governor for life
July 8, 1675, his appointment to go into effect on the death or
resignation of Berkeley.

Colonel Jeffreys performed the duties of the office for about
eighteen months, when he died. Sir Henry Chicheley, Knight,
described by some as " an old and crazy gentleman," but in fact,
as shown by his private and official life, an estimable man, then
acted as deputy governor until the tardy Culpeper arrived in
May, 1680.

Culpeper did not relish a sojourn in Virginia, and the king
had to threaten to supersede him if he should longer delay his
departure from England. He was subsequently dismissed for
absenting himself from his government without permission,
after being warned for committing a first like offence. It
was during his last absence from Virginia, in May, 1682, while
Chicheley was deputy governor, that the tobacco plant cutting
occurred. There being a surfeit of tobacco, and its culture consequently being unremunerative, the people asked that an Act
of Assembly should be passed forbidding its planting for a year.

[*] *Calendar of State Papers*, 1677-1680, p. 776.
9—J. T.

This request not being granted, the people set about destroying the crop. " The frenzy " spread from plantation to plantation throughout Gloucester and New Kent Counties, the owners of the destroyed crops joining the mob and assisting in destroying those of their neighbors. Both sexes participated in the movement, and when the authorities put a stop to the proceedings in the day time, it was resumed at night. Major Robert Beverley was accused of being the instigator of the trouble, and upon his arrest it practically ceased. When Culpeper returned to Virginia he tried several of the culprits and, under a musty old law of the time of Elizabeth, hanged two of the poor creatures.

Governor Culpeper resided, during his incumbency, at Berkeley's old home, Green Spring. Of the mansion scarcely a trace remains, while the spring flows unceasing, probably as profuse and cold as it was over two hundred years ago.

One of Culpeper's acts, while governor, was to defraud the English soldiers sent to Virginia during Bacon's Rebellion, out of part of their pay by paying them off in pieces of eight, the coin current, at a higher value than that fixed by law, and appropriating the difference to his own uses.

Culpeper was superseded by Francis, Lord Howard of Effingham, in August, 1683. Effingham did not arrive till February, 1684, and meanwhile Nicholas Spencer, secretary of the Council, acted for him. During Effingham's administration the state house, burned in 1676, was rebuilt, and a treaty made with the Five Nations in New York (August 5, 1684), who, for many years, had been a constant menace to the settlements in Maryland and Virginia.

Lord Howard established the reputation of being about as avaricious and unscrupulous as Lord Culpeper. He endeavored to have an act passed empowering him and the Council to raise money for the expenses of the government without the approval of the Assembly, but was unsuccessful. He was perpetually engaged in controversies with the Assembly, and was extremely unpopular.

During about two years of Effingham's term while he was

absent, between 1688 and 1690, Colonel Nathaniel Bacon, Sr., president of the Council, acted as governor. No events of particular moment occurred in the colony during this period.

In June, 1690, Sir Francis Nicholson, Knight, as lieutenant-governor, assumed the reins of government for Effingham. He was tactful and conciliatory, and made an excellent governor during his two years of office. Governor Nicholson was one of the subscribers to, and founders of, William and Mary College.

In 1692, Sir Edmund Andros, Knight, succeeded Effingham as governor. He was also appointed representative of the Bishop of London, of whose diocese Virginia formed a part. The Rev. James Blair, first president of William and Mary College, had been appointed the bishop's commissary, or representative, several years before. A clash over ecclesiastical matters occurred between the governor and the commissary, in which although the governor, on account of his official position, had a temporary advantage, he was finally worsted. In November, 1698, Nicholson returned to Virginia as governor and successor to Andros. His second administration was the antithesis of his first, and in it he distinguished himself for committing numerous petty illegal acts instigated by spite or caprice.

During Nicholson's second term Jamestown's career was terminated by the seat of government being transferred to Williamsburg.

Few of the Royal governors seated at Jamestown ran the gauntlet of office and escaped without meriting censure. Some of the governors under the London Company were probably the most meritorious, not the least of whom was the illustrious La Warr. Although La Warr's stay in Virginia was of too short duration to fully test his ability and character, it must not be forgotten that he not only bestowed his talents, but gave life and fortune as well to the founding of this nation.

THE ENGLISH AND VIRGINIANS OF THE SEVENTEENTH CENTURY

A S the reign of James I. of England began but four years before the first landing of the English at Jamestown, and as that of his great grandaughter, Queen Anne, terminated fifteen years after the capital of the colony was transferred to Williamsburg, the life of the town was approximately coincident with the Stuart dynasty. It is more nearly measured by the reigns of the four Stuart kings.

Virginia was ever loyal to the house of Stuart. When the tocsin of civil war sounded, the impetuous and courageous Berkeley prepared for resisting the invasion of Virginia by the "Roundhead" forces. Then, too, at the restoration, Virginia was in the van in welcoming the king to his own again.

Although a knowledge of the physical characteristics of Jamestown and its environs are necessary to mentally depict its outlines, it is also essential, to make the picture life-like, to give some account of the conditions existing during its time. Unfortunately, Jamestown held no Evelyn or Pepys, from whose journals to cull, and for information we, perforce, must turn to the "Mother Country."

As many of the Jamestonians were from London and its vicinage, a presentation of some of the more important social and economic conditions prevailing in England, especially at the metropolis, during the reign of the Stuarts, should in a measure give an idea of conditions that obtained during the same period at Jamestown.

At the opening of the seventeenth century the dawn of enlightenment was beginning to break on the Christian world, and England was furnishing her quota of scholars, whose efforts contributed towards lifting the dark veil of superstition that enveloped the earth, by unfolding the laws of Nature and

KING CHARLES THE SECOND

KING JAMES THE I st

KING CHARLES THE FIRST

Nature's God, and turning them to the advantage of mankind. The seed planted by the writings of Francis Bacon, John Locke, Sir Isaac Newton, and others, however, was slow to bear fruit. The emancipation of the human mind was gradual, and the benign light of knowledge did not shine with sufficient strength to fully dispel the encumbering mist until many years after the little town had sunk into its sleep, which knew no awakening. Coincident with the promulgation of a knowledge of the Copernican system, Astrology was thrust aside; but the flames hitherto kindled by fanaticism under the guise of religion still claimed their victims at the stake in the persons of heretics, witches and sorcerers.   King James I participated in the torturing of thirty unfortunates, who were executed at Edinburgh, to wring from them confession of a witch conspiracy against him and his newly wedded wife, Anne of Denmark. The savage law of executing witches was practiced, to a considerable extent, in the Massachusetts colony, where, at the instigation of the Rev. Cotton Mather, nineteen so alleged were executed in 1692. In Virginia, none was executed, but one poor creature was abused by ducking. But then, as Bancroft explains, "New England was a religious plantation."

Inasmuch as when ships were delayed by stress of weather or through fault of their masters or crews it was the fashion to ascribe such bad fortune to the presence of a witch among the passengers, one of whom was singled out and summarily executed, it was rather hazardous in those days for a homely woman of advanced years to take passage for Virginia. There is record of two women bound for Virginia being thus hanged at sea, Mary Lee in 1654 and Elizabeth Richardson in 1658. John Washington, brother of Lawrence, witnessed the execution of the latter, and endeavored to prevent it.

Until near the close of the century the almost sole means of communicating intelligence at a distance was private correspondence. News letters were in vogue, and a few poor newspapers were being printed in London, but a newspaper at all resembling one of to-day did not appear till about the time of

Queen Anne. The first weekly newspaper published in England,
" The Newes of the Present Week," made its first appearance
May 23, 1622, or the day following the first massacre of the
Virginia settlers by the Indians.

The education of females was, as a rule, neglected. Some
women of high social standing could not write their own names.
Books were scarce and expensive. The profit and enjoyment of
the writings of Shakespeare, Locke, Dryden, Bacon, Milton, and
others, were restricted to a few, possessed of considerable means.

The seventeenth century passed without giving England a
single painter or sculptor of renown. A landmark of the times,
however, St. Pauls, or " Paules " as it was familiarly called,
survives at London, a perfect creation of its style, by one of
England's greatest architects, whose tomb carries as part of the
significant epitaph, " Si monumentum requiris, circumspice."
Wren's constructive genius and talent as an architiect shone out
in the rebuilding of London after the great fire of 1667, when,
among other works, he constructed fifty of the fifty-three
churches that were rebuilt out of the ninety-eight that were then
consumed. It is said that he designed some of the early Virginia buildings, but there appears to be no evidence to support
this statement.

Medical science was in an almost negative state. True, the
circulation of the blood had been discovered by Harvey, but the
skill of the general practitioner of the healing art appeared to
have been of the highest who surrounded the compounding of
his prescriptions with the greatest mystery, and could produce
the most startling and nauseous concoctions. Medical works
there were, some home written, others translations, but with the
exception of some still familiar simples, such as senna, gentian,
wormwood, rhubarb, and a few other dainty herbal remedies,
they contain few prescriptions that would not arouse our com-
miseration for the unhappy patients to whom they were administered, or that would reflect credit even on an Indian Medicine
Man, or an African conjurer. Poultices made of toads and
snails were highly regarded, and when King Charles II was on

his death bed, suffering apparently from a stroke of paralysis, besides the placing of hot irons to his head and subjecting him to the almost invariable bleeding, he was forced to swallow a brew made from human skulls. No wonder he complained of a consuming fire within.

A feature of the treatment of fever consisted of covering the patient with bed clothes, almost to suffocation, in a closed hot room, and John Evelyn notes in his journal his belief that one of his children was killed by this treatment.

Among the great army of medical quacks and empirics there were a few bright lights. All, however, resorted to bleeding, except for loss of appetite and a few other ailments. Shortly before the middle of the century the learned Sydenham proposed using for fevers Peruvian bark, but recently introduced into Spain (1642). In this, however, he was opposed by his confrères. Touching by the sovereign for the cure of King's Evil, dating back to the time of Edward the Confessor, was practiced till the reign of Queen Anne.

Although religious fanaticism was not as violent in the seventeenth century as in the sixteenth, the penalty of death at the stake was still inflicted on those adjudged heretics by ecclesiastical courts. This penalty was meted out to two Arians in the reign of King James I, four years after the settlement of Jamestown. The conflict between religious sects still obtained, it being the fashion for the dominant sect to persecute and torture those whose theology or creed was at variance with its own, and to use harsh and cruel measures in pointing out the road to salvation.

Sympathy for those in misfortune was not generally manifested, as it is to-day, and the few charities lacked organization. The rabble made sport of the felon on his way to the gallows, and followed him with gibes and execrations. The culprit in the stocks was derided and pelted, and could account himself fortunate if he survived the ordeal with no worse punishment at the hands of his fellows than the bodily bruises made by their missiles, and the laceration of his feelings by their taunts. This ɪack of feeling was not confined to the lower classes, for we are told that gentlemen of fashion showed a like moral depravity by attending by way of pastime the whipping of women prisoners in the jails.' Men's minds had not been directed into humane channels, and the standard of benevolence was at such a low ebb that some who were accounted philanthropists thought it not amiss to employ children of the tender age of six in factories. Discipline in the school room, the family, and in military organizations, was harsh and cruel.

Tennis, golf and card games then, as now, were pastimes, also morris dances and May pole games, both now all but obsolete. About a quarter of a century after Jamestown was founded the Puritans in some districts of England prohibited the people from engaging in games and sports on Sundays, in consequence of which King Charles I issued his " Declaration of Sports," forbidding any interference on Sunday afternoons with those indulging in such sports, as dancing, archery, and other similar pastimes, provided they had attended divine service in the morning. Bull baiting and playing at bowles, however, were prohibited. The play of skittles was abolished by law.

During the reigns of James I and Charles I music was regarded as a necessary accomplishment for both sexes, and was cultivated by all classes. Chappell tells us that " Tinkers sung catches, milkmaids sung ballads, each trade and even beggars had their special songs. The bass viol hung in the drawing-room for the amusement of waiting visitors, and the lute, cithern and virginals were necessary furniture of the barber shop. They had music at dinner, * * at supper, * * at weddings, * * at funerals, * * at night, * * at dawn, * * at work, * * and at play." Under the Commonwealth, music was condemned by the Puritans as frivolous, and as one of Satan's snares, and they excluded it from the church and family. With the Restoration, music was revived. Madrigals, resembling glee songs; dramatic plays, interspersed with music, called

---

' *Macaulay's Hist. of England*, Vol. I.

KING WILLIAM THE THIRD

QUEEN MARY

KING JAMES THE SECOND

masques, the precursor of the opera, were the common forms of presenting it. The harpsichord, as successor of the virginals, appeared during the century, but the musical instruments in more common use included violins, viols, and several forms of harps and wind instruments.

The purchasing power of the English laborer's wages, compared with the prices of necessaries, was apparently about half as great as to-day. The wage rate was fixed by law, and employers paying a higher one were subject to penalties.

Wheaten bread was too expensive for general use, and pease pudding, oatmeal porridge, rye bread, cheese and small beer, were common articles of diet. Meats, as compared with wages, were high. Vegetables in common use, both in England and in Virginia, comprised peas, cabbage, cauliflower, onions, turnips and carrots. Tea was introduced into England towards the end of the Commonwealth, and coffee in the sixth year of King Charles the Second's reign.

It was not until seventy-two years after the landing of the English at Jamestown that the act of Habeas Corpus, which in a restricted sense had become a statute in the reign of Charles I, received, in a more extended form, royal approval at the hands of Charles II. James II endeavored, although unsuccessfully, to have Parliament repeal the act. The act was not operative in Virginia during the Jamestown period.[5]

When the colonizing of Virginia was begun it is authentically stated that there were nearly 300 offences against the law for which the death penalty, with or without the benefit of clergy, was prescribed. Among them was the refusal of the accused to plead in court. A notable instance of the infliction of the penalty for this offence in the Colonies was that of Giles Cory, pressed to death "between boards" at Salem, Massachusetts, in 1692. Witches and sorcerers were to pay their reckoning without benefit of clergy, also those who should "relieve comfort or maintain any Roman Catholic ecclesiastic," or who were seen

---

[5] *Campbell's History of Virginia.*

consorting with Gypsies for one month. Conviction of theft from a church, dwelling, or the person, of the value of twelve pence, constituting compound larceny, of breaking a dam entailing the loss of fish, of cutting down a cherry tree in an orchard, of transporting wool, lead or silver out of the realm, of counterfeiting and of breaking jail, were also to be atoned for by death, although the culprit in these instances was accorded the privilege of receiving from his priest the solace of religion. Even beyond the middle of the 18th century 160 of these relics of the jurisprudence of a still lightless age remained unrepealed, among them being the burning at the stake of women who had murdered their husbands. This penalty, derived from an ancient Druidical law, was not repealed until the reign of George IV.

An example of the excessive penalties then inflicted is illustrated by the case of Wm. Prynne, a Presbyterian lawyer, whose offence consisted of having written a book against the stage. His work was entitled " Histriomastix, or a Scourge for Stage Players." It was published in 1633. The penalties were a fine of ten thousand pounds sterling, Prynne also to have his ears cropped and his nose slit, to be disbarred, branded in the forehead, to stand in the pillory in Westminster and Cheapside, and be perpetually imprisoned, " like monsters that are not fit to live among men nor to see the light." Judging from the inventive genius displayed in devising punishments, the bent of men's minds appeared to have been fiendish, rather than human.

Few of the twenty-four Lord Chief Justices of the King's Bench serving under the four Stuart kings, possibly six, can be classed as eminent for ability, learning and high character, and still fewer exhibit the characteristics usually ascribed to the personality of an ideal judge. Of the six worthy judges, five were dismissed, among them the illustrious Coke, for being disinclined to carry out the nefarious and arbitrary whims of their sovereign masters. The other eighteen were sycophants of various degrees of unfitness. Persons of known bad character were sometimes appointed to this exalted position, a case in point being John Popham, chief justice in the reigns of Elizabeth and James I. While Popham attended the Middle Temple, and after he was admitted to the bar, he was a member of a gang of highwaymen, who replenished their purses by night on Shooter's Hill, near London, at the expense of belated travelers. It appeared to be essential for the holding of this high office that the incumbent should render a servile compliance to the king's will. Persons having the additional characteristics of being arbitrary and remorseless were sometimes sought and found. A Stuart never retained on the bench a justice of "doubtful principles," and the giving of a judgment or opinion against the Crown was tantamount to inviting dismissal.

In the reigns of Charles II and his brother James II, the principal purposes of the courts appear to have been oppression and revenge. The juries were packed by the minions of the court, and the defendants were almost invariably found guilty. In conducting a court it was not uncommon for the chief justice to browbeat and intimidate the witnesses, insult and defame the accused and coerce the jury into rendering a verdict in accordance with his wishes, regardless of the testimony.

At the beginning of the seventeenth century the resources of England were not sufficiently developed to maintain its population, although it was probably only about one-fifth of that of to-day, and many there were to whom, on account of the prevailing small daily stipend of sixpence to a shilling, Virginia offered great inducements as a haven from interminable poverty. To such the prospect of becoming landed proprietors seemed sufficient recompense for a few years' service to the London Company, or to those of ample means who advanced their passage money, to be repaid in land grants and the service of the person thus indentured.

The majority of the Virginia settlers naturally were from the more humble walks of life, including many of the sturdy yeomanry. Virginia also received a large number of the gentry, and many bearing titles. The last named generally held official positions. There were also large accessions to the colony in the persons of political exiles, many of whom as officers and soldiers, had participated in the several revolutions of the seventeenth century. Thus, after the fall of Drogheda, in Ireland, many of those not put to death by Cromwell's soldiers were exiled to Virginia. Again, after the battle of Worcester, 1600 soldiers of Charles I's army followed. After the Restoration, many nonconformists and Cromwellian soldiers were exiled to the colony, and some of these took an active part in the semi-religious uprising of 1663, and in Bacon's Rebellion. A number of Scotch prisoners of war were deported after the uprising in 1678, as well as some of the participants in Monmouth's Rebellion in 1685. Some malefactors were sent to Virginia, but then, as has been shown, offences which in those days were felonies involving the death penalty are to-day rated but as mis-demeanors. Sir Thomas Dale, while lieutenant-governor, advo-cated sending felons to Virginia, but his methods of governing were those of a harsh centurion and taskmaster, and were well adapted to incorrigibles. Children were kidnapped, sold into slavery and sent to Virginia, until this crime was made a capital offence, without benefit of clergy.

Charles II ordered the Virginia officials to suspend the opera-tion of the law which had been enacted in 1671, prohibiting the introduction of " jail birds," but the Virginia colonists pro-tested, and probably to some purpose, against their country being made a " Botany Bay."

The lives led by the Virginians of the seventeenth century, according to to-day's standard were comfortless and monoto-nous. There was nothing to amuse, divert or entertain the mind, except the arrival of an occasional vessel from across seas or from neighboring plantations and the gossip furnished by the meeting of the Assembly or the holding of court.

The volume of money in circulation in the colony until the latter part of the seventeenth century was very small, and en-tirely inadequate for business purposes. The standard of value was tobacco, as gold is to-day. As the value of tobacco in Eng-lish money varied with its demand and supply, it was a most unsatisfactory medium of exchange. Bills of exchange, based on the holdings of Colonial merchants in England, appear to have circulated somewhat in the same manner as our bank-notes of to-day.

Communication between distant points was carried on almost entirely by boats. Horses were scarce for about the first half of the century, and coaches were very rare, even at the close of the century. Lady Berkeley is known to have had one, for it is recorded that she induced her husband, Sir Wm. Berkeley, to employ the common hangman, a negro, to act as driver of the chariot which was offered to the commissioners to take them to the boat landing after their call at Green Spring to bid Sir William farewell, shortly before his departure for England in May, 1677.

An enterprise which furnished occupation and great expectations to both poor and well-to-do people in Virginia was the raising of silk. Much time and care were expended to make it a success, but despite persistent and repeated efforts, it failed to give compensating returns. The settlers failed to understand that the climate of Virginia is too damp and changeable for silk culture, which conditions were the real bar to the industry. Edward Digges, one of the Cromwellian governors, according to the inscription on his tombstone, was the sole proprietor of silk raising in Virginia. Sir William Berkeley, as stated in another chapter, also took an active part in the enterprise.

The attempts to manufacture glass were unsuccessful. Beads were made for trading with the Indians, and were the exclusive property of the London Company. The sand at Jamestown, however, proved to be unsuitable, the glass workers became dissatisfied, and the manufacture was abandoned.

As the dwellings were small and families large, the sleeping chambers were overcrowded in early colonial days. Governor Berkeley's house at Green Spring had but six rooms and a hall. The James River mansions and others that survive were erected in the eighteenth century, many years after Jamestown had passed away.

Table ware was generally of pewter. Table forks were by no means in general use. Towards the end of the seventeenth century table silver and plate were used in the households of the wealthy. Mrs. Elizabeth Digges, widow of the governor, left at her death what to-day would be regarded as a fair supply of silver plate for a person of moderate means. That cooking utensils and house furnishings were scarce is evidenced by the bequests in wills of iron pots and feather beds.

Brass utensils were largely used in the kitchens of the wealthier. Paintings of merit were apparently rare.

Although a lady of wealth usually possessed a fine silk and flowered gown for state occasions, also a lace trimmed bonnet, a gold or gilt stomacher, and ornamented fan and other finery,* wardrobes were rather scant, and the articles composing them were for utility rather than display.

The distinctions of class, which were so well defined among the early settlers obtained although in a gradually diminishing scale, till long after the American Revolution. Preferment for official position depended largely on social prestige, rather than on aptitude or merit. The lower social order was humble, at first, almost to servility.

The conditions attending Southern plantation life fostered the Cavalier spirit among the proprietors. From this order, after losing a large measure of the hauteur common to its autocratic forbears, was evolved a type famed for its dignity and lavish hospitality, " The Old Virginia Gentleman."

Frontier life, in which, for a bare existence, a strong arm and a brave heart were required, taught the settlers, even of the most humble class, self-reliance and fearlessness, and developed that latent love for complete freedom which is planted by the Divine hand in the bosoms of the English people. From this class principally, at a later day, came the rank and file of Bacon's followers, in his trying marches through marsh and forest in

---

* *Economic History of Virginia in the 17th Century*, by Philip Alexander Bruce.

quest of the hostile savage, and to defy a tyrannical governor. From this class also, still later, sprung the hardy pioneer, who made it his mission to penetrate the unexplored regions beyond the Virginia mountains and build up an empire of vast proportions reaching to the furthest western limits defined in the second charter to "the first colony."

APPENDIX.

AN ABRIDGED DESCRIPTION OF THE METHOD EMPLOYED IN LOCATING "THE NEW TOWNE," FROM THE VIRGINIA LAND PATENT RECORDS.

The following patents were used for locating "the New Towne:"

(1) John Pott, "Doctr, of Physicke," for three acres "in the new Towne," dated August 11, 1624.

(2) Same grantee, for 12 acres, including the above three acres, dated September 20, 1628.

(3) John Phips, for 120 acres, "part thereof in James Citye's liberties," dated February 23, 1656. This patent includes 12 acres "formerly granted by patent unto Dr. John Pott."

(4) John Knowles, for 133 acres, 35 9-10 chains, "part within and part without the liberties of the said city," dated May 6, 1665.

The tract covered by this patent includes the above 120 acres purchased from John Phips; 3 acres 44 37-100 chains, also purchased from said Phips; and 9 acres 71 53-100 chains, "due for transportation for one person."

(5) William Sherwood, for 308 acres in James City and James City Island, dated April 20, 1694.

The Sherwood tract included 3½ acres "purchased by him the said Wm. Sherwood of John Page Esqr;" 1 acre (see (9) below; 133 acres 35 9-10 chains "being heretofore granted by patent dated the 6th day of May 1665 to one John Knowles;" 28½ acres "granted by patent dated the 4th day of October, 1656, to one John Bauldwin;" and the remainder, "being formerly granted to Richard James by patent dated the 5th day of June, 1657."

(6) Henry Hartwel' for 2 acres, 1 rood, 24 1-10 poles, dated April 20, 1689.

[144]

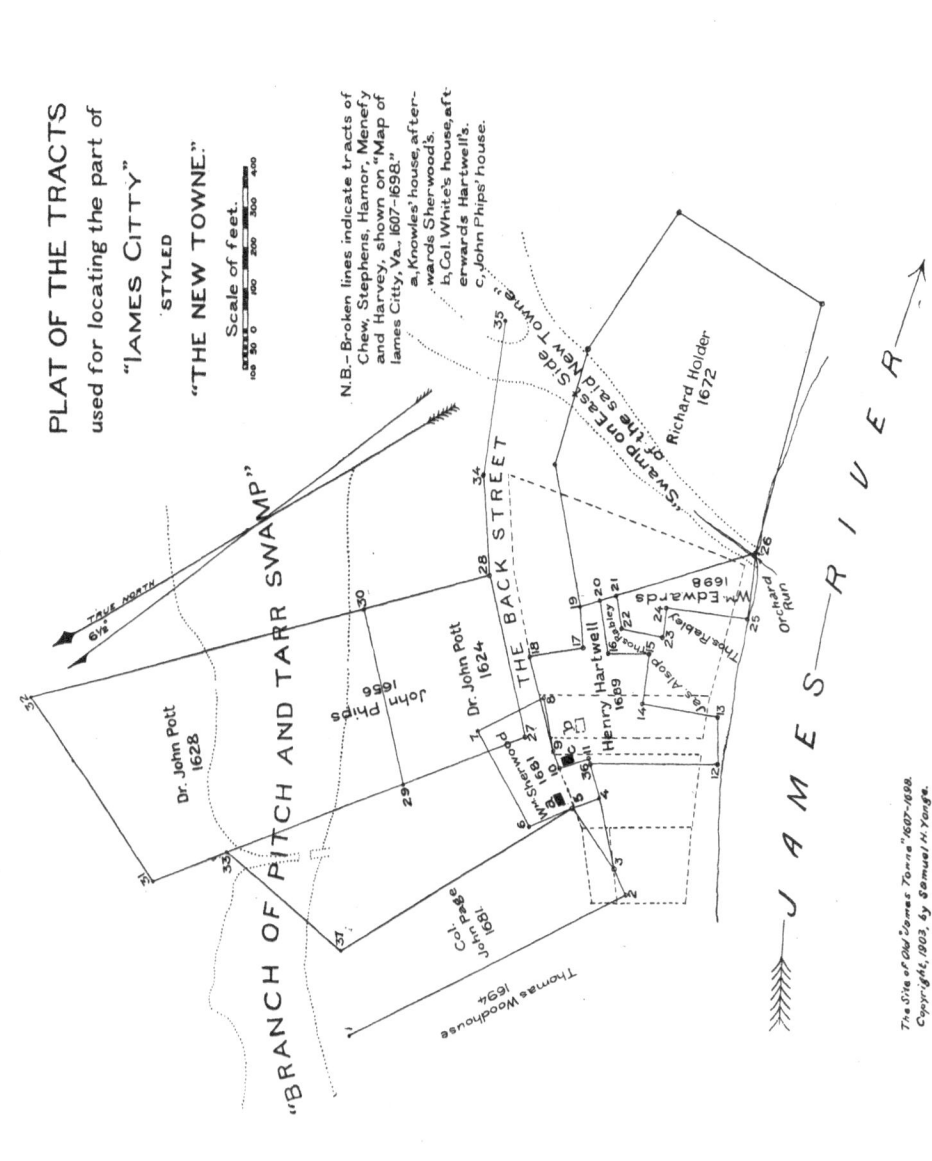

PLAT OF THE TRACTS
used for locating the part of
"JAMES CITTY"
STYLED
"THE NEW TOWNE."

Scale of feet.
100 50 0   100   200   300   400

N.B.– Broken lines indicate tracts of
Chew, Stephens, Hamor, Menefy
and Harvey, shown on "Map of
James Citty, Va., 1607–1698."
a, Knowles' house, after-
wards Sherwood's.
b, Col. White's house, afterwards Hartwell's.
c, John Phips' house.

TRUE NORTH
6½°

"BRANCH OF PITCH AND TARR SWAMP"

Dr. John Pott
1628

John Phips
1656

Dr. John Pott
1624

Col. John Page
1681

Thomas Woodhouse
1694

Wm Sherwood
1681

Henry Hartwell

THE BACK STREET

Tho⁵ Alsop

Tho⁵ Bagnley

Tho⁵ Rabley

Wm Edwards
1698

Orchard Run

Richard Holder
1672

"Swamp on the East
Side of the said New Towne."

JAMES RIVER →

The Site of Old James Towne 1607–1698.
Copyright, 1903, by Samuel H. Yonge.

(7) Richard Holder, in " James Citty," for 8 acres, 1 rood, 5 poles, dated January 28, 1672.

(8) Wm. Edwards, Jr., for 127 poles in James City, dated October 15, 1698.

(9) William Sherwood, for one acre of land * * * " in James Citty on which formerly stood the brick house formerly called the Country house," etc., dated April 23, 1681.

The tracts represented by the patents are shown on the accompanying " Plat of the Tracts." They were connected by means of their common boundaries, as follows:

(1) The northern boundary of the Pott tract, (2) line 31-32, is also one of the lines of the Phips (3) survey.

(2) The line 31-32 is also common to Phips (3) and Knowles (4), and the line 31-33 of Knowles is a part of the line 31-27, of Pott.

(3) The lines 4-11, 11-10 and 10-9 are common to Knowles (4) and Sherwood (5).

(4) The lines 4-11, 11-10 and 10-9 are also common to Sherwood (5) and Sherwood (9).

(5) Lines 11-10 and 10-9 of Hartwell are common to Sherwood (5), Sherwood (9) and Knowles (4), and Hartwell 36-11 forms part of line 4-11 of each of the above tracts, (5) and (9).

(6) Line 19-20 Hartwell (6) differs $1\frac{1}{4}°$ in azimuth from the line 19-26 of Holder (7). The length of the line 19-20, however, being but $51\frac{1}{2}$ feet, the above difference of azimuth would change the position of the point 20 but one foot, a too insignificant difference to be considered in a compass survey. Hartwell's patent reads for the course 17-19, " buts on the land now or late of holder." It also reads for line 19-20, " thence along holder," showing that the above line is a part of Holder's western boundary.

(7) The azimuth of the line 19-26 of Holder (6) is the same as line 21-26 of Edwards (8). The length of the above line for the Edwards tract, however, is shorter. The south end of the above eastern boundary of the Edwards tract (8) is described as being " at ye mouth of ye Orchard Run on James River," and

the same end of the line for the Holder tract is described as being " at high water mark on James River side at the mouth of a small run entering thereinto." The runs are undoubtedly one and the same.

The patents show that Orchard Run was on the south bank of the island. As there is but one stream entering the river on that bank that could be designated a run, it was readily identified.

The descriptions in the patents furnish some other data as to the names of owners of adjacent land, which further confirm several of the above determinations.

Several errors were discovered in the survey notes of the transcripts of the patents above referred to and, until they were located and corrected, it was found to be impracticable to plat the tracts. The errors were those of the surveyor and of the scrivener who transcribed the patents. They comprise principally the reading of the south end of the needle by the surveyor, and in transcribing, misplacing the decimal point in the length of a course given in figures, and entering azimuths incorrectly.

In one of the patents, (Sherwood 9), the azimuth of every course of the survey is reversed. The last named tract might be omitted from the plat, as it only serves the purpose of confirming the junction of three other tracts, Knowles (4), Sherwood (5) and Hartwell (6), which is well established.

All of the foregoing tracts being platted, the point 26 was superposed on the mouth of Orchard Run, previously identified and located on a modern map, and the map as made up from ancient patents rotated around point 26 until its magnetic meridian had a western declination of 6½ degrees.[1] It was then found that point 1 of Sherwood (5) fell on the south side of the

[1] The magnetic declination at " James Citty " about the middle of the seventeenth century was probably six or seven degrees west. There are no data prior to 1694 for any better than a rough approximation. Six and a half degrees appears to be close enough for the class of surveys to which is here applied.

branch of "Pitch and Tarr Swamp," thus agreeing with the description in the patent record for Sherwood (5). Another point of Sherwood (5) near its eastern end, omitted from the accompanying plat—as by including it the map would have been made too large—falls within thirty-five feet of where the description places it, viz., on the edge of a great marsh on Back River.

A causeway across the swamp before referred to, being probably the bridge given as a witness mark in the Knowles patent (4) being found very near the point indicated by that patent also confirms the location of "the New Towne" as exhibited on the map.

The south line of the Pott tract 27-28, (1) and that of Phips (3) fix the position and direction of Back Street. The southern boundaries of tracts of Hartwell (6), Holder (7) and Edwards (8), fix the positions of parts of the southern bank of the island for the seventeenth century, which is thereby found to conform closely to that of to-day, thus showing that it has not been abraded to any extent by the waves. This is as it should be, for the part of the island, shore immediately below the present wharf has not been greatly exposed to wave action. The ancient south shore of the island and the positions of the Pott tracts and the Back Street being established, the Ralph Hamor tract was platted by its dimensions given in the patent records.[2] Its position was then approximately arrived at by finding by trial the place on the chart where the length of the tract would fit in between the Back Street and the "highway along the banke of the Main River."

The area of the plat of John Harvey[3] being given, also its northern boundary, Back Street, its eastern boundary "the Swamp lying on the East side of the said New Towne," its southern boundary, "upon the highway close to the banke of the Main river," the approximate position of the tract was ascertained after several trials.

---

[2] Va. Land Pat. Record, Book I, p. 3.

[3] *Ibid*, Book I, p. 5.

From the descriptions of the Harvey and Hamor tracts the position of those of George Menefy[4] and Richard Stephens,[5] and also those of the two cross streets, all of which are mentioned in the descriptions of the two first named, were readily found, and finally the tract of John Chew,[6] all as shown on the " Map of Iames Citty, Va., 1607-1698."

N. B.—Lines indicated on the " Plat of the Traces " by numbers 1, 2, 3, 4, 11, 10, are part of Sherwood (5) survey.

Lines indicated by numbers 9, 10, 11, 4, 5, 37, 33, 31, 32, are part of Knowles (4) survey.

Lines indicated by numbers 28, 34, 35, are part of Phips (3) survey.

The dwellings of Knowles, later Sherwood's, of Col. White, later Henry Hartwell's, also that of John Phips, although having no connection with the matter of locating the " New Towne," are shown on the plate, on account of being interesting features. Their positions were determined from references to them in the patents.

By comparing the " Plat " with the " Map of ' Iames Citty,' " especially the Pott and Holder tracts, the relation of the two plates will be apparent.

" Back Street " appears to have lost its name before 1656, as Phips' patent of that year, although following its lines, does not refer to it by name. Charlestown's (Boston) " Back Street," dating from very early colonial times, survives under its original name.

---

[4] *Ibid,* Book I, p. 4.

[5] *Ibid,* Book I, p. 1.   [6] *Ibid,* Book I, p. 7.

NOTE.

The Ambler MSS. and "The Site of Old 'James Towne,' 1607-1698."

By the publication in April, 1904, of the report of the librarian of the Congressional Library, for the fiscal year of 1903, the author of " The Site of Old ' James Towne ' " was apprised of the acquisition by the library of a collection of MSS. of which he had no previous knowledge, showing the former possessions of the Ambler family situated principally at Jamestown or in its vicinage. An examination of the papers was made by him towards the end of April.

The collection comprises upwards of 140 MSS., consisting of original patents, deeds and leases, copies of other similar documents, certified and uncertified, and copies of three wills, also several plats of surveys, all showing the chain of title of the lands as vested in different owners up to 1809, and, in one instance, dating back to 1649. There is no reference in the Ambler papers, however, to grants of the tracts which formed the "New Towne" in 1623. A comparison of some of the original patents in the collection with their transcripts in the land register's office at Richmond shows that the latter, in the main, are correct, and have been properly interpreted, thus proving the accuracy of the " Map of ' Iames Citty,' 1607-1698." As however, there is no plat of Jamestown among the Ambler papers, their possession at an earlier day would not have lessened the labor and study required for constructing the above map and the " Plat of the Tracts."

The papers comprising the collection contain evidence confirming the composition of the turf fort, and show that parts of it were still standing in 1721. They also confirm some other important features of the map.

Among the collection are several skeleton plats of surveys, two of which relate to Jamestown. One, made in 1680, shows that the western shore line of the island in the 17th century above the " Pitch and Tarr Swamp " was about as shown on the author's map. The agreement of the above chart with the " Map of ' Iames Citty,' " in this respect, indirectly confirms the position given on the map of the part of the western shore of the island below the upper branch of the swamp. This evidence greatly strengthens the view expressed in the monograph as to the site of the landing-place at Jamestown of the first band of settlers. It is evident from the other skeleton plat that the Sherwood tracts of 1681 and 1694 were situated with regard to each other and the branch of Pitch and Tar Swamp, as drawn on the ". Map of ' Iames Citty,' Va., 1607-1698," and the " Plat of Tracts." These coincidences corroborate the position of the Pott tract as given in the map, and indirectly show the general correctness of the part of the map for the east end of the town.

A reference in a lease for land on the second ridge in 1693 confirms the location of the third and fourth state houses on the third ridge, as established from other data. No light, however, is thrown on the location of the church by the Ambler papers.

It is learned from William Sherwood's will that the epitaph on his tombstone is worded in accordance with his instructions to his principal legatee, Sir Jeffrey Jeffreys, Knt., of London.

Interesting information is supplied by the Ambler papers regarding the 3½-acre tract of " Col. Jno. Page of 1681," shown on the " Plat of the Tracts." The site of this tract on the " Map of ' Iames Citty ' " is covered by Sir Francis Wyatt's lot, and the lot attributed to Captain Roger Smith.

The Page tract included the original grant from Harvey to Richard Kemp, Esq., in 1639, who conveyed it to Wyatt. Wyatt, through his agent, Wm. Pierce, sold to Sir Wm. Berkeley, who sold it to Walter Chiles, whose widow—afterwards Mrs. Susan Waddinge—sold to Colonel John Page, who conveyed it to Wm. Sherwood in 1681. The concluding sentence in the description of the survey of the tract made for Sherwood

Patent to William Sherwood, Gent, for 308 acres including part of site of "James Citty," in 1694. Signed by Governor Andros, witnessed by R. Wormeley, secretary
[From the Ambler MSS. collection]
[About one-half actual size]

in 1682 reads: "Including ye Ruins Sq^r Kemps Old Brick House." The above house was the first brick house built at Jamestown. It was 16 by 24 feet in plan and was referred to by Gov. Harvey in 1639, with considerable pride, as being the fairest that ever was known to the country for substance and importance. By the locating of the Page tract, therefore, the site of the first brick dwelling house in Virginia becomes approximately known. The evidence, though slight, shows that the house was near the southwest corner of the Page tract.

Ralph Wormley, while secretary of state, resided on the Page tract, on or very near the Kemp grant.

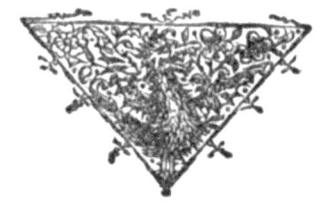

www.ingramcontent.com/pod-product-compliance
Lightning Source LLC
Chambersburg PA
CBHW020640180626
46816CB00003B/1063